Frank Andrew Munsey

Derringforth

Frank Andrew Munsey

Derringforth

ISBN/EAN: 9783337024956

Printed in Europe, USA, Canada, Australia, Japan

Cover: Foto ©ninafisch / pixelio.de

More available books at **www.hansebooks.com**

DERRINGFORTH

By FRANK A. MUNSEY

VOLUME TWO

NEW YORK
FRANK A. MUNSEY & COMPANY
1894

DERRINGFORTH.

XLIII.

IT was with a thrill of pleasure that Marion recognized Derringforth as the ferry boat and steamer drew close together. She quickly attracted his attention. He looked at her for a minute, and then, with chilling indifference, turned away. It was a deliberate cut, it seemed to her. She was deeply chagrined.

"It is all I could expect from him," she said to herself with flushed cheeks. "It is quite in keeping with his rudeness in not answering my letter or coming to see me before I sailed. I can't understand why he treats me so."

Her heart had glowed with sympathy for him a few moments before; now it was like ice. She declared indignantly that she would never give him a chance to snub her again.

"His action is simply inexcusable," she went on. "I don't know what his grievance is, but whatever it is he ought to have a little sense. I detest such stubbornness. He wasn't like this in the old days.

The change in him is unaccountable. It is fortunate for me that mama took the stand she did. I should have had a delightful life if I had married him—a man with such a disposition. And I rebelled against mama's wishes. I never can thank her enough for her firmness."

Marion was justified in the feeling that swayed her, believing as she did that Derringforth recognized and deliberately cut her. The burst of indignation was natural. It was also feminine.

The steamer swung in to the pier. Marion's spirits were deeply depressed. She looked cautiously down upon those who had assembled to greet their returning friends, hardly expecting, after her experience with Derringforth, to see a smile of welcome for her. But there was one, and it was a smile that would have touched the heart of any girl.

The mingled look of surprise and delight that flashed to Marion's face repaid Burton Edwards a thousand fold for the traversing of a continent. The ardor of his love had not been dampened by a score of failures to win her hand. He and Derringforth were utterly unlike. They were good types of distinctly different temperaments. Edwards had always been able to discover some cause that had prevented him from securing her promise. He was satisfied that she was upon the point of giving it at a dozen different times, but something had always happened to prevent her from doing so.

Derringforth would not have deceived himself in this way. He would never have allowed his heart to blind his eyes. Little things, that meant nothing to Edwards, had a world of meaning for him. He saw in them a glimpse of purpose—a trend that Edwards could not detect. At one time it was a telegram that prevented Edwards from securing the prize, as he thought. At another it was Derringforth who stood between him and Marion. Later it was Richard Devonshire, then a duke, an earl, and a dozen other ardent European admirers.

"But with Marion in America it will be different," Edwards reasoned. "There is Derringforth, to be sure," he went on, "but why should I fear him?" He tried to persuade himself that he need not, but he was not altogether successful. He knew nothing of the present relations between Derringforth and Marion. He was satisfied that they were not engaged. Had they been, she would not have permitted the attention she received in Europe. This was something tangible to which he could cling. But a feeling of uneasiness disturbed him, nevertheless. He had seen Derringforth but once. He knew very little of him. Marion had never talked of him. This fact, in itself, was significant, to say the least.

The account of Derringforth's downfall was a startling piece of news to Edwards. A throb of sympathy went out from his heart toward his fallen rival.

His nature was too generous to rejoice in another's

misfortune, and yet he was human. He could not help appreciating the situation.

"The gods are with me this time," he reflected. "The coast was never so clear before."

He was on the pier long before the steamer reached it. Marion's look of delight, when she saw him there to welcome her home, thrilled him with a delicious sense of happiness. He could hardly restrain the impulse to clasp her in his arms when he took her hand, but this was a liberty he dare not take.

Marion had said good by to her friends in Europe with deep reluctance. They had done everything for her pleasure. It had been one great holiday. She turned her face toward home with many misgivings. Burton Edwards was in California, and Derringforth —well, he was in New York, but would he come to see her? Her other friends were not to be counted upon — not that they had forgotten her, but time scatters with a ruthless hand. Some had married, death had claimed its share, others had left the city, and yet others had formed new ties.

Marion felt, therefore, that she would find no one to welcome her home. She had merely mentioned incidentally, in a letter to Burton Edwards, the day on which she would sail. That he would be the first to take her hand in friendly greeting on arriving in America never entered her mind.

She was standing by the rail as the ship neared her dock, and was looking down upon the eager faces of those on the pier. Suddenly she caught a glimpse of Burton Edwards. She was startled for an instant. Then came a thrill of pleasure. It was a delightful surprise. For the moment, at least, he was immeasurably Derringforth's superior. If Edwards had planned everything to his own liking, it could not have been more to his advantage.

XLIV.

STANLEY VEDDER tried very hard to look pleasant when Dorothy joined him and Nellie on the tennis court, but he could not wholly disguise his feelings. He was anything but happy. Derringforth's presence at the Rayburns' had made him wretched. He had wished a thousand times that it had been his leg instead of Derringforth's that was broken. He had no special fondness for broken bones, but anything was preferable to having Derringforth in Dorothy's very home.

Vedder was in love with Dorothy. She had a certain fondness for him. Sometimes she fancied it was love. If it were, it was very mild. They had known each other a long time. There was no spontaneity in her admiration for him, if admiration it was. None knew this better than he. He would have rebelled and quit the chase long ago with any other girl who responded so indifferently to his suit. But Dorothy Rayburn was a prize. He dare not assume the independent tactics, and to remonstrate would, he feared, cut him off altogether. He chafed under this condition of things. At times, when he was alone, he gave full vent to his feelings. There was a bluish shade in the atmosphere on these occasions.

Vedder's family was good. That is to say, the average was good. There had been some members of it in past generations who went wrong, but there were others whose high standing and excellent attainments did much to atone for the shortcomings of their kinsmen.

Stanley's father had been one of the promising Vedders, but his career was cut short. He fell a martyr to the cause of the Confederacy. The Vedders had been people of large means up to the time of the war. They owned many slaves, and had extensive investments in Virginia and other parts of the South. The war swept away their fortunes. Stanley's mother had very little property left.

Captain Vedder and Colonel Rayburn grew up from boyhood together, and together they entered the army. The one was taken; the other was spared. Colonel Rayburn felt that he owed a duty to the widow of his dead friend. He interested himself in her affairs, and managed them so well that she was enabled to live comfortably and had the means to give her son a college education. But when she had done this, she had gone to the extent of her ability. His four years in college had cost vastly more than she expected. Her entire surplus, beyond the reserve necessary for a living, had been expended on him.

She had given him the money cheerfully, believing that he was fitting himself for a career which would be the realization of that splendid future which his father had planned for himself.

Young Vedder learned during his college days the pleasures to be derived from the expenditure of money, and with a taste for these pleasures—a taste remarkable for its rapid development—he resolved to have money. A resolution of this sort costs nothing. It is easily made. The words trip lightly on the tongue. But the getting of money means something vastly different. Vedder had never earned a dollar in his life. He knew nothing about work, save that it was something to be avoided if possible. He seemed to know this intuitively.

But there are other ways of getting riches than by the sweat of the brow. A great many ingenious methods have been tried, first and last, with varying degrees of success; but the one that seems most in favor with the present generation is marriage. Occasionally a man who resorts to this plan discovers that he has made a woeful miscalculation. The scheme is not without risks, notwithstanding its present popularity. Not infrequently the procurer of wealth by this means finds that the rate of interest he has to pay is something astounding. But when the mortgage is once on a man it is rarely lifted except by death. It is supposed to be a life transaction. The terms of the contract run that way.

But now and again a man is lucky enough to love where the golden eagles lurk. This is rare, to be sure, yet there are such cases. Vedder's was one of them.

He had been at home over four months now. His ostensible purpose in remaining there was study, while his actual purpose was that he might be in daily touch with Dorothy. There was, however, another cause for his not going away that had a good deal of weight with him—a cause that meant nothing more nor less than the making of his own living. Money getting was a problem to which he had given little thought. It bored him. There was a flavor of work about it that he detested. And, moreover, no opening had been presented to him. This was strange, to be sure, for was he not a college graduate, and had he not won distinction on the field of sports? The fact remained, however—the cold, clammy fact, that no house had as yet invited him to join its management. Thus much in justification of his idleness.

But Vedder's summer had not been wasted. He felt that he had made actual progress with Dorothy, but this progress had been won at a frightful cost of dignity. The necessity of smiling when he felt like swearing—the realization that he was the plaything of a girl's imperious fancy and that he dare not rebel—all this soured him.

Dorothy delighted in nothing so much as in teasing him. It is a trait in girls that is quite universal, to torture the man who will submit to their teasing.

Vedder cursed the fates that he was not rich, feeling that if he only had money he would snap his fingers defiantly in Dorothy's face. But now he must humiliate his soul and look pleased—look as if he enjoyed the pangs of jealousy and the many other annoying phases of the situation; and all this that he might in the end marry Dorothy.

All went comparatively well with him, however, until September, when Nellie Bradwin arrived on the scene. Two girls together, if they, or either one of them, be disposed to tease a man—and one or both are very likely to be—can torture him fifty times as badly as one alone. This may not be the exact proportion. The estimate, however, is under rather than over the correct figure. Nellie's presence, therefore, gave Dorothy a wider scope, but it was not until Derringforth's arrival that she had the opportunity to tease Vedder to her heart's content.

Dorothy's heart bounded with a wicked little bound as she thought of the fun she could now have at Vedder's expense. "I ought to be very nice to Mr. Derringforth any way," she said to herself in justification of her attention to him. "He is papa's guest, and I should certainly try to make it just as pleasant for him as I can."

"You are breaking Stanley's heart, Dorothy, by flirting so with Mr. Derringforth," said Nellie.

"How absurd you are," replied Dorothy. "I am not flirting."

"What do you think Stanley would call it?"

"Oh, well, he gets jealous so easily, you know."

"And that is just why you delight in teasing him. But suppose you were to get Mr. Derringforth in love with you?"

"What nonsense you talk, Nellie."

"I am not so sure it is nonsense."

"Why, Mr. Derringforth will only be here a day or two. When he gets back to New York he will forget that he ever knew me. And this is such an opportunity for teasing Stanley—he is so absurd."

To sum up the situation, then, at the end of Derringforth's first day at the Rayburns', it must be recorded that there was every evidence of a well ordered flirtation already begun between him and Dorothy. But a flirtation with the daughter of Colonel Rayburn is the last thing Derringforth would have dreamed of. He had deluded himself with the idea that he was done with girls forever. There was a certain negative contentment in his soul that he did not wish to be disturbed. He had had an experience that satisfied him. He prided himself on the feeling that he knew when he had had enough. He was out, and he proposed to stay out. But he had been at the Rayburns' a few hours only when he found a certain delight in Dorothy's presence that he could not get from books or sports or business. Why shouldn't his heart have responded to a girl so sweet? He was yet in the early twenties. His soul had been starved for two years. It was in part a self imposed starvation. He had steadfastly refused to meet girls, but now that he had been entrapped, as it were, into the presence of one, and such an one, he could no longer choke back all feeling of sentiment. It bounded up in his heart, and for the first time in many months contended with his will for the mastery—that will that had ruled with an iron hand.

Derringforth's reserve receded, and a light came into his eyes that had not shone there for many months. Dorothy's smile was food for his half famished soul. He had no thought of flirting with her; he had no thought of love. He simply relaxed his stern vigilance and allowed himself to live once more; allowed his heart to drink deep of the joys that God intended for man and provided for him in the creation of woman. Dorothy's presence satisfied a longing that had cried out within his soul for many and many a day—a longing that had been starved into subordination but not unto death. A strong, vigorous nature like Derringforth's cannot be converted into cold indifference simply by force of will. It may be saddened and quieted by sorrow or by some dreadful shock, but the fires of youth cannot be quenched by these. Time and illness and death alone extinguish them.

What appeared, therefore, to be a flirtation on Derringforth's part was in fact no flirtation at all. He was never more serious. But with Dorothy it was quite different. Her motive has already been revealed. Beyond the desire to make herself agreeable to her father's guest, her aim was simply to tease Vedder, who foolishly permitted himself to be teased. She was not flirting then. She was acting a part, and acting it so cleverly that no canons of good taste were outraged.

Derringforth, of course, was ignorant of her motive. He appreciated her attention. It pleased him—delighted him. Then came the race, the fall, and the broken leg. Everything was changed in a twinkling. Dorothy thought no more about teasing just then. She blamed herself for Derringforth's accident. The thought of her responsibility sobered her. She was very sorry for what she had done. It made her heart ache to see him suffer, and she did everything possible for his comfort and pleasure by way of atonement. The attention that she gave him before his accident was continued, but in quite a different spirit. She sang and played for him by the hour, and in one way and another made herself indispensable to his happiness.

She had no thought of love in connection with Derringforth. Whatever she did for him was prompted by pure kindness and by the desire to make amends in so far as possible for the wrong she felt she had done him. He did not hold her responsible for his accident, and hadn't the remotest idea that she blamed herself for it. She felt like a culprit in his presence, and was almost impelled at times to confess what would have opened Derringforth's eyes and quickened the old cynicism into new life. But the confession was not made. Day by day she began to fill a larger place in his heart. On one pretext and another he managed to keep her with him more and more as the time flew by.

Vedder saw this, and was desperately depressed. He was ignorant of Dorothy's secret motive in her devoted attention to Derringforth. He could put but one construction upon it, and that construction was torture to him. And Dorothy, moreover, was very serious now. The old spirit of teasing seemed to have left her. Vedder cursed the hour that brought Derringforth to the Rayburns'.

Dorothy found herself instinctively comparing the two men. Girl as she was, she could see a world of difference between them. Derringforth commanded her respect. She had no desire to tease him as she had teased Vedder. The thought of such a thing almost frightened her. She read him intuitively, and she read him well. It is interesting to note the effect of different natures upon a person. No two have precisely the same influence; no two awaken the same desires and impulses. One man will bring out the sweetest and best that there is in a woman; another will make her a shrew. Certain types of character in man and woman—in man and wife, make a perfect whole.

The tension was wearing on Vedder. He felt that he was losing ground. Dorothy seemed to be drifting further and further away from him. He would gladly have submitted to her teasing now. That was infinitely preferable to neglect. There was no intentional neglect, however, on Dorothy's part. It was merely comparative. With the time she gave to Derringforth it could not be otherwise. She was not conscious of any change in her feelings for Vedder, and yet there was a shading of disgust in her heart at his jealousy. Once or twice she made up her mind to tell him how foolishly he was acting, but there never happened to be a good chance to do so. The shadow on his face deepened, and that shading in her heart became bolder.

XLV.

One day Vedder came to take Nellie to drive. This was a change of tactics. Dorothy came out on the veranda and chatted gayly with Vedder. He was annoyed. His scheme evidently had not produced the effect on her he had hoped for. His aim was to awaken a sense of jealousy. If she felt at all cut up she certainly disguised her feelings well. But she was quite capable of doing this. None knew it better than he.

Dorothy watched the carriage disappear around a bend in the road, and then she went in and drummed on the piano. Her mind was not on her playing. She was thinking—wondering why Vedder had slighted her. She had expressed delight when Nellie told her of the invitation. She was sincere in what she said. But that was then. Now, she fancied that she would feel a little bit better if she had had a chance to refuse the invitation. It was not that she cared about the drive. Vedder's ruse was not wholly without effect, but she was bound that he should never know it.

"I don't know why I should care one way or the other," she said to herself. "He hasn't been at all nice to me lately."

Her playing was very erratic. At times it revealed almost a gloomy frame of mind. The notes reached Derringforth's ear. He listened and wondered. That it was Dorothy's touch there could be no doubt. What had happened to produce this depression? He puzzled his brain for an answer. Presently the music ceased altogether.

Dorothy had gone into the library. She picked up a partially finished book and began reading. The theme was that one which is ever fresh. Love never fails to awaken a sympathetic response in the human heart. Poets have sung of it; novelists have written of it, and the millions of the earth, since man was man, have been swayed by it, and yet it is as new and sweet and all absorbing as when it first thrilled the hearts of Adam and Eve.

Dorothy was soon lost in the story. She was nearing the end. The author was realistic. Page after page teemed with sentiment. The heroine was so sweet, so refined, and so fair withal, that Dorothy was fascinated with her. The hero, it seemed to Dorothy, was not unlike Derringforth. Her eyes flew over the printed words, gaining momentum as they slid from line to line. The scene grew in intensity. The book trembled in Dorothy's hands. Her face was white. It was a supreme moment. The climax was reached suddenly. Two hearts beat as one. The story was finished. The end came abruptly.

Dorothy longed for more. Her soul was attuned to love. To start another book now would be like falling from heaven to earth. She could not do it, and yet she must do something. She went out on the veranda, and looked down the winding roadway to see if she could see Vedder and Nellie. They were not in sight. She walked up and down the piazza, and gazed off toward the mountains in the distance. The reflection from the soft, fleecy clouds that hovered over them was very beautiful. The November sun sent its slanting rays across the valley. The varying shadows, shading into a deep, dark background on the hillsides, presented an attractive picture. But these did not satisfy Dorothy. She was not in the mood to enjoy inanimate nature.

She thought of Derringforth. An almost irresistible impulse possessed her to go to him, and yet she hesitated. What excuse did she have for disturbing him? He might be sleeping. She thought of a dozen good reasons why she should keep away from him, and then—well, it was scarcely a minute later and she was beside him.

"I have been wishing you would come," said Derringforth, his face brightening.

"Are you very sure of that?" she replied, with a look of half doubting inquiry.

"I am indeed. Certainly you cannot doubt me."

"I was afraid you wouldn't wish to be bothered by me."

"It was your absence that bothered me. I have been actually blue."

"I can't imagine that of you."

"Neither could I have imagined until today that you ever fell into a gloomy mood."

"Why, what do you mean?" asked Dorothy, her cheeks flushing.

"Tell me all about it. You have made me anxious."

Dorothy became just a little confused. Derringforth smiled at her embarrassment. "I am actually curious now," he added.

"Why do you assume that I was gloomy?" asked Dorothy.

"Won't you sit down? I don't want to lose you now that you are here. Don't you see how I have brightened up since you came in?"

"You are evading my question," said Dorothy. Derringforth's words had begun to satisfy the longing that had impelled her to come to him. The shadows of depression had vanished from her face. She had the faculty of always being graceful. Her head rested on the high back of the chair. It was inclined slightly to one side. Her position was easy and picturesque. She was just so far away from Derringforth that he could see her to the best effect. The open door leading into the sitting room was a little to her left. The soft light sifted in through the blinds and was reflected toward her. Derringforth's eyes told of his admiration.

"Why do I assume that you were gloomy?" said Derringforth. "I didn't assume it; I knew it."

"You knew it?"

"Yes, this is the time I read your thoughts, you see," laughed Derringforth.

Dorothy looked puzzled. "Won't you tell me how you read them?"

"Yes, if you will tell me how you read mine regarding that race—you know you promised to do so."

"You are driving a sharp bargain, but I suppose I shall have to tell you," answered Dorothy, and she repeated what Derringforth had said while coming out from under the influence of ether.

"Upon my soul, this is taking an unfair advantage of me," declared Derringforth, "to etherize me and then hold me responsible for utterances made while in that condition."

"But you practically admitted that what you said was true."

"How did you learn what I did say?"

"Papa told me."

"I shall have to have a reckoning with your father when I see him. He should not place me so at your mercy."

"Have I been very hard with you?" There was mischief in Dorothy's eyes.

"Very hard," answered Derringforth with assumed seriousness. "I have never been so completely ruled as by Miss Rayburn."

"I'll tell you what it is, if you won't call me Miss Rayburn any more I will be just as nice to you as I can be."

"What shall I call you, then?"

"What is the matter with Dorothy?"

"I shouldn't dare call you that."

"Why not?"

"What would your mother say?"

"I will tell her that I asked you to call me Dorothy."

"Are you serious?"

"Certainly. Miss Rayburn—why, it is so formal—makes us seem like strangers."

"You would rather not think of me as a stranger?" queried Derringforth, looking steadily into Dorothy's eyes.

Her cheeks burned crimson. "I couldn't quite think of you in that way," she answered.

"Not when I have gone back to New York?"

"Would a separation of a few hundred miles make you think of me only as a stranger, or perhaps forget me altogether?" she asked.

"No, I could never forget you, Dorothy," he said.

Her eyes were cast downward as she answered: "I am very glad you have concluded to call me Dorothy."

"Did I call you that?" replied Derringforth. "I was thinking of you, not your name."

"But you will continue to call me Dorothy?"

"Yes, on one condition."

"And what is that?"

"On the condition that you call me Phil."

"Oh, but that wouldn't do."

"You call Mr. Vedder Stanley."

"But I have known him all my life."

"And that, you think, makes a difference?"

"Yes, don't you?"

"Yes."

"Then why impose such a condition?"

"Because it seems to me I should not call you Dorothy unless you are equally familiar with me."

"I think there is a difference. You are older than I; then, too, you are a man—a city man, and are accustomed to formality."

"But all my friends call me Phil, why not you?"

"You really want me to?"

"Certainly I do; it would make me feel entirely at home."

"I shall accept your condition, then. Papa said we must make you feel at home. This lodges the responsibility with him, you see. But do you know, you haven't kept your side of the agreement yet—I mean about the reading of my thoughts. I believe you changed the subject purposely."

"Positively I did not. We drifted away from it,"

answered Derringforth. Then he explained about the piano playing and his interpretation of it.

"I shall not allow you to hear me play any more," said Dorothy.

"That would be cruel," returned Derringforth, looking hurt.

"I can't help it. I'm not going to have you interpret my moods."

"I might not always do so. But today it was so plain I couldn't help it. Won't you tell me what made you so gloomy?"

"I wasn't exactly gloomy. I didn't pay any attention to what I was doing. I was simply drumming away and thinking what I should do to kill time. Nellie had just gone to drive."

This admission set Derringforth thinking. What was there in connection with Nellie's drive that should make Dorothy gloomy, he asked himself? He did not divulge his thoughts.

"I wish I were in shape to take a drive," he said.

"How I wish you were," replied Dorothy, with her usual enthusiasm.

"Would you go with me?"

"Certainly I would. Won't you please hurry and get well so that we can take some of the lovely drives about here before the roads get muddy?"

"The thought is extremely tempting," answered Derringforth, "but you know if I were able to go driving I should be able to be in New York."

"But you wouldn't have to go right away."

"It would be criminal in me to remain away from my office longer than is absolutely necessary. I am sure you know something of my failure."

"It was too bad, and you had made such a fortune. But papa says you will come out all right. He has great faith in you, Phil."

Derringforth felt a choky sensation in his throat. There was something in the way she spoke—in the word *Phil* as it left her lips—that touched him.

There was a moment's pause, and then he said: "I suppose your cousin went with Mr. Vedder?"

"Why do you suppose that?" asked Dorothy quickly.

"Oh, it was merely a fancy," answered Derringforth indifferently.

"No, you can't put me off that way."

Derringforth laughed at Dorothy's persistence.

"Now just tell me your reason," she continued.

"What sort of a reason would you like? If I must manufacture one I want it to suit you."

"Well, then, you might say it is because you think Stanley and Nellie are in love with each other."

"How did you know I thought that?" returned Derringforth, surprised.

"'Oh, it was merely a fancy.'"

"Well, I am certainly convinced of one thing."

"And that is?"

"And that is that it is not safe for me to think any

more. I am sure I have not said anything that should have led to such an inference."

" But don't you know," laughed Dorothy, " that men have a way of looking what they think ? "

" Some men may."

" And you fancy that you are an exception ? "

" I did entertain that notion, but I think my conceit is weakening."

" That is delightful—anything but a conceited man. But tell me seriously what led you to think Nellie and Stanley were in love? "

" I got the idea the first day I came," returned Derringforth, and then he proceeded to tell her of his impressions during that first afternoon's ride.

Dorothy burst out into unrestrained laughter. " This is awfully funny," she said.

Derringforth actually blushed. " I can't quite see where the fun comes in," he rejoined.

" The joke is that you should think you were making Stanley unhappy by riding with Nellie."

" It is evident that I was mistaken."

" Why, surely you were."

" They are not in love with each other, then ? "

" No, not the least little bit."

" I must acknowledge that I read people very badly. I have been deluding myself all this time. But tell me one thing," continued Derringforth. " How was it that Vedder came to change from you to Miss Bradwin when we began the descent of the hill? "

"I think you and I started off together," answered Dorothy, her cheeks flushing. Derringforth's eyes were very keen. Dorothy's heightened color meant something to him.

"Now you are evading my question," he said. The flush on her face deepened. "In a word," he continued, "wasn't the stop a mere ruse of Vedder's to get back with Miss Bradwin?"

"You are very uncomplimentary to me," said Dorothy, with an injured air. "Did you find me so dull that you would have liked to desert me?"

"Indeed I did not. I was delighted with the change, and have been congratulating myself ever since on my good luck. But I'm not going to let you off in this way. You have not answered my question."

"Oh, that is so, but you ask so many questions—are all New York men as curious?"

"This won't do," returned Derringforth. "I shall assume that your answer is in the affirmative."

"You must not assume anything of the kind; and besides, it would not be correct."

"It would not be correct?"

"No."

"Then the ruse was yours."

"Mine?" exclaimed Dorothy in a manner that was intended to mislead.

"I can't figure it out in any other way."

"Think of what that means, and it was only

just now that you told me your conceit was leaving you."

"I admit the charge," laughed Derringforth. "I should be willing to admit almost anything, I am so delighted at the discovery I have made."

Dorothy's protestations were ineffectual. Derringforth had got at the truth, and she could not blind his eyes.

"You might as well admit it," he said. "It was very sweet in you. I shall bless you all the years of my life for the pleasure of that afternoon."

"You wouldn't have had this broken leg, though, but for that."

"And but for this broken leg I should never have known you as I do now."

"I am afraid that is a very poor compensation," answered Dorothy.

"On the contrary, it is a priceless compensation. You have been a revelation to me. I had become very cynical before meeting you, and seeing the sweet home life I have found here. I am beginning to believe that the loss of my fortune was a blessing in disguise. I might never have known you, otherwise."

"I thought it was only old men who have suffered disappointments and have been buffeted about, who become cynical," replied Dorothy.

"The calendar does not measure a man accurately," answered Derringforth. "Some men at twenty are older in all that goes to make up life than others at a hundred."

"But your life can't have been so very hard," rejoined Dorothy. "Just think of all the money you have made, and you are so young!"

Here was Derringforth's opportunity to tell Dorothy of the affair that had very nearly ruined his life. The words were almost on his tongue. He hesitated. "Not just now," something whispered. The impulse was gone. He could not bring himself to the point again. It were well for him had he told her.

The rumble of wheels was heard.

"Stanley and Nellie are coming," said Dorothy, "I must run down and meet them." She got up to go. Derringforth put out his hand and took hers.

"I wish you were not going, Dorothy," he said. "Must you go?" he added, looking into her eyes. His tones were those of love. Her hand was white and soft. He pressed it to his lips. The temptation was more than he could resist.

It was a moment of delirium for both Dorothy and himself. Her heart was too full to protest. She flew from him—almost literally flew. Her soul was lighter than the air. She was in her own room. The impress of his lips was still upon her hand. Each throb of her heart was intoxication.

A creak of the stairs warned her of some one's approach. She shot a hurried glance at the mirror.

Her cheeks were ablaze. The door opened, and Nellie came in. Dorothy tried to appear natural, but the effort was a failure. Nellie's quick eye interpreted well. The revelation was not wholly a surprise. She had read Dorothy during the past weeks better than Dorothy had interpreted herself. She had seen from day to day unmistakable evidence of growing interest in Derringforth. She had tried to discourage this tendency, both as Vedder's ally and because she herself did not admire Derringforth. Vedder's antipathy for him had influenced her. By numerous suggestions and innuendoes he had poisoned her mind against him. The feeling was slight at first, but it had developed, under the tutelage of Vedder, into positive dislike—a dislike which had within the last hour become contempt. The discovery, therefore, she had made since returning from her drive, filled her with anxiety for Dorothy.

Nellie was glad she was there, so that she might undertake the rescue of her cousin from a man not worthy of her love. Derringforth had suddenly become very black in Nellie's eyes. This intensified feeling was due to information she had gained during her drive with Vedder. They had been out but a little while when it became apparent to her that he had something of unusual importance on his mind. He began by making an incidental reference to Derringforth.

"It will not be much longer that we shall be

obliged to have him with us," said Nellie, speaking as if his departure would be a welcome relief.

"It will be a fortunate day for all concerned when he is gone," returned Vedder. There was something in the way he said this that meant even more than his words.

"Why, what do you mean?" asked Nellie quickly.

"There are times," replied Vedder significantly, "when it is not quite wise to repeat all one knows."

"I hope you have no reason to distrust me," said Nellie, looking slightly hurt.

"On the contrary," returned Vedder, "I have every reason to trust you, but this matter bearing on Derringforth is one that I don't like to be mixed up in. I regret the possession of information that has come to me. To be sure, I was in a way instrumental in getting it. I merely mentioned Derringforth's name incidentally in a letter to a friend in New York, asking, as one naturally would, if he knew him, or something of the sort. I don't remember my exact words. The reply from my friend is one that I little expected, I assure you, and, as I said, I wish I were not in possession of the facts he sent me. My interest in the Rayburns, as you know, would naturally lead me to protect them from evil associations. But this is an exceptional case. Mr. Rayburn himself brought Derringforth into his home, and he naturally feels under obligations to him on account of the accident. Of course, when he invited Derringforth to spend a day or two with him, he did not foresee this accident, and accordingly did not dream of a prolonged stay. But what could he do other than permit Derringforth to remain in his home under the circumstances?

"It was a case of necessity—of humanity—and Mr. Rayburn, as you know, is one of the most generous of men. My position is an extremely delicate one. I would do anything in reason for the Rayburns; no one knows this better than you do. You can readily understand, then, my feeling—my dread of touching a matter of this kind. Of course, if I had received no letter from my friend, I should be ignorant of Derringforth's true character, but now I realize my responsibility to the Rayburns and to you. I don't know what to do, though. I know what I ought to do, but I shrink from doing it. I can't bring myself to the point of mixing myself up in a disagreeable matter like this."

By the time Vedder had finished this speech Nellie was wrought up to a point of intense anxiety. She implored him to confide in her, and finally declared that she would not allow herself to remain in the same house with Derringforth another night unless she knew just the kind of man he was.

This pressure—this extreme pressure—made Vedder yield, apparently much against his will.

That portion of the letter bearing on Derringforth ran as follows:

Do I know anything of a man named Phil Derringforth? Yes, I know *of him*. His name is rather familiar to New Yorkers just now. He recently failed for something like two million dollars. How strange that you should have been thrown in with him, and how infernally odd that he should be laid up down there in Virginia with a broken leg just at this time. Is it a genuine break? It is hinted in the Street that it is not—that it is a sharp dodge to enable him to keep away from New York for the present. It might be a little stormy for him here now. This is the idea expressed by one of our customers—a Mr. Burrock. I happened to remember seeing Derringforth in our office one day with Burrock, and it occurred to me that he could give me some facts about Derringforth that might interest you. I accordingly invited Burrock out to luncheon with me today. He was quite free to express himself about Derringforth. In a word, he evidently has a very poor opinion of him.

He claims that all the money Derringforth ever made was made on his advice. He says that Derringforth is simply a plunger. Finally he went back over Derringforth's history and told a most romantic story of a desperate love affair that came near killing him. It was this, I gleaned from Burrock, that drove him into the reckless ways that have characterized his career in the Street. Burrock thinks this affair turned his head and ruined him. He has no social position, so far as I can learn. When I asked about his moral standing Burrock smiled suggestively. This will give you a sort of outline sketch of Mr. Derringforth, and with these facts before you, you can answer the question yourself as to whether he is the sort of man you should know. I have thought it better to tell you what I could learn of him, rather than assume the responsibility of advising you. It is not necessary for me to add that he is not an acquaintance of mine.

This letter was written by a college chum of Vedder's, Minton Varnum, who had entered his father's office soon after graduation. Varnum & Company were stock brokers. Burrock had recently begun dealing with them. They were also Van Stump's brokers, and it was through him that Burrock went to them.

This letter from young Varnum contained nothing very serious against Derringforth. It would not have appeared so to the normal mind, but Nellie's mind was not normal as regarded Derringforth. It was in such a state that she was prepared to believe anything about him so long as it was against him. Vedder had seemed to regard the disclosure with horror. She readily fell into his way of looking at it. The situation appeared very grave. What was to be done— what should she do? This problem engrossed both her attention and Vedder's throughout the remainder of the drive. She came home deeply troubled. A disagreeable duty devolved upon her. She realized the delicacy with which she must discharge it.

Nellie remained with Dorothy but a few moments and then went into her own room. Dorothy was left alone with her thoughts. She was glad to be left alone. The presence even of Nellie grated on her nerves. It was the first awakening of genuine love in her soul. It was a revelation; it was life. The feeling was as unlike that which she had had for Vedder as the soft air of June is unlike the chill winds of December. She was too happy to think connectedly. The world had suddenly taken on a new beauty. The atmosphere was sweet scented.

She went to her window and looked out across the valley and off to the mountains beyond. The sun had sunk behind them. They were in deep shadow. Dusk was hovering over all. The mist was rising from the low lands. It was the same scene Dorothy had looked upon an hour before, but now darkened by approaching night. There was little in it then to awaken a sense of pleasure in her heart, but now it was radiant with beauty. Its transformation had been complete.

The light of day faded. The landscape was shut out. She still stood by the window, peering into the gloom. But it was not gloom to her eyes, for she was not alone. Derringforth was with her, and his presence illumined all the world.

She dressed for dinner; she dressed for Derringforth. Nellie was in the parlor, reading, when Dorothy came in. She glanced up from her book; the book fell from her hands. The fairest flower of the Old Dominion was before her. One look, and her arms were about Dorothy. It was an outburst of admiration. Now more than ever Nellie dreaded the task she had undertaken to perform.

Mrs. Rayburn was ignorant of the happiness that added so much to Dorothy's beauty. There was a light in her eyes, an élan in her manner, that her mother had never seen there before.

When dinner was over Nellie drew Dorothy aside. She began in a roundabout way to approach the subject of Derringforth's blackness. Vedder would despise her if she weakened. Finally the critical point was reached. The color had faded from Dorothy's face. The letter was in her hand.

XLVI.

THE evening passed by, and Derringforth did not see Dorothy. The morning came and went. The day dragged on, and still she did not come to him. He had thought until his brain reeled, trying to discover some cause for her absence other than that he had offended her. But this was the only explanation that suggested itself.

"What shall I do?" he groaned. "What can I do? If I were anywhere else it would not be so bad, but to be in her very home, and under such obligations as I am to her family, makes it a thousand times worse. If I could only get away—indeed I can't stay here. How shall I explain? There is no explanation—none except one. But that would not help me, for I have no right to love her, situated as I am. She will hate me for what I have done—and Mrs. Rayburn and the colonel!"

Derringforth covered his eyes with his hands and shuddered. He tried to stop thinking, as each thought added to his torture. He might as well have willed himself to be in the furthermost parts of the earth, and opening his eyes have expected to find himself there.

"I wonder what they will do with me?" he went on, moving about restlessly. "I shall be sent away, of course. Colonel Rayburn is doubtless on his way here already. He will be very angry. I wish I had never—no, a thousand times no, I would rather suffer any torture than never to have known Dorothy. Wherever I am, and whatever my condition, I can still think of her as I have seen her here— can still love her as I have loved her here."

Mrs. Rayburn went away early that morning to spend the day. Derringforth knew nothing of this. Her absence gave intensity to his morbid fancies. He had not seen any one but servants since Dorothy fled from him with the impress of his lips upon her hand. Not even Nellie had come to him. Derringforth stood it as long as he could. He rang for a servant and sent him off with a note to the doctor, asking him to come at once and "fix him up" in some way so that he could take the night train for New York.

The old surgeon smiled cynically when he had finished reading this urgent appeal, and after indulging himself in the utterance of a few choice nuggets of profanity prepared to go and see if Derringforth had gone stark mad. He met Mrs. Rayburn on the veranda. She had just returned home. "What does this mean?" he asked, handing her Derringforth's note.

Mrs. Rayburn read it hurriedly. "I am sure I don't know," she answered, becoming suddenly anxious. The doctor started to say something in keeping with his feelings, but wisely checked himself.

"Something has happened in New York," ventured Mrs. Rayburn. "Perhaps he has told Dorothy. I will call her."

"Nothing could have happened that would warrant him in making such a fool of himself," returned the gruff old doctor as he disappeared through the door. A minute later he burst in upon Derringforth, and in a vernacular rather more fierce than elegant said: "What in the devil is the matter with you, young man—have you gone mad?"

"You must judge of that yourself," answered Derringforth. "Call it anything you like, if you will only fix me up so that I can take the train tonight."

"Come, come, no more of this raving; do you want to be a cripple all your life?"

"All my life!" repeated Derringforth, as though the future had little interest for him. "Let us deal with the present," he added. "I have a reasonably clear idea of what I wish. Can you do for me what I have asked of you?"

"I will give you a dose that will make you sleep for a week instead, sir," growled the old doctor with a fierceness that was not intentional. "And, sir," he continued, "if I hear any more of this ranting about New York I will keep you here on your back all winter—I will, upon my head, I will."

"I simply must get away tonight, and that is all there is of it. If you can do for me what I asked of you, all right; otherwise I shall endeavor to get away without your assistance."

"Stuff, stuff," retorted the crusty old surgeon, feeling Derringforth's pulse. "You have worked yourself up into a fine nervous condition," he went on. "What does this mean?"

Derringforth hesitated for a minute and then replied: "I suppose I might say that it is due to my anxiety to get away."

"You might say that you are an ass," stormed the old doctor.

"Yes, I might well say it," returned Derringforth, feeling that the words were especially applicable to him just then.

"Good," said the old man, rubbing his bony hands together in grim delight. "This is the first rational thing I have heard you say. You are not so mad as I thought."

XLVII.

DOROTHY was in her room. She had scarcely left it since reading the letter that Nellie had brought her from Vedder. The disclosure was a rude shock to her young nerves. The reflections on Derringforth's character and habits as a business man, had that been all, would have made her his champion. But the thought that he had loved another was a cruel wound, just then when her whole soul throbbed with the first awakening of passionate love.

A few hours before she would have seen nothing very black against Derringforth in the letter; now she saw enough to break her heart. She threw herself upon her couch, buried her head in the soft silken pillows, and sobbed bitter tears. Everything had become suddenly black and drear. The night wind whistled shrill through the trees. All that was bright and sweet and dear in life had vanished.

Nellie tried in vain to comfort her. As well might she have sought to quiet the fury of a tempest by gentle words. Strong feeling, stirred to its depths, must, like the tempest, spend itself.

The morning came, and the sun burst upon the world and flooded it with light and warmth, but these did not reach Dorothy. With her the fierceness of the storm had passed, but the day was as somber and chilly as the night. That fresh young love that had come into her heart a few hours before was bruised and bleeding.

Up to this time she had been swayed by impulse alone. Her powers of reasoning had been paralyzed by a tremendous shock, but now she began to think rationally. This was natural. It evidenced a healthy mind, and a healthy mind, if it be at all analytical, is pretty sure to go to the bottom of things—to reason out the why and wherefore.

Thought filters the dark waters and brings within range of the eye things that were hid. Gradually Dorothy's vision penetrated deeper and deeper. The day had not advanced very far when she began to discover the outlines of Vedder's motive. It was almost too much to believe—almost more than she could realize, that Stanley Vedder would lend himself to such perfidy. This revelation aroused in her the strongest feeling of contempt for him, and at once made her Derringforth's champion. Her sense of justice alone would have inspired this feeling, had there been no other incentive within her heart. Not long after arriving at this stage Dorothy was very busy making excuses with herself for Derringforth's shortcomings.

There is nothing so keen sighted as love; there is nothing so blind. It can discover virtues and merits and shadings of merit that the most powerful microscope would not reveal to the normal eye. It can penetrate beyond the ugly, angular lines and see beauty and gentleness and sweetness. It can find ample and palliating cause for vicious tendencies and vicious acts; and yet this same power of penetration —these same love inspired eyes, are dull to defects— dull to absolute blindness.

The letter that Vedder had inspired was carefully phrased, so that it would not betray his hand. There was nothing on the surface that would in any way criminate him. It was beneath the surface that Dorothy saw his shadow stealthily approaching Derringforth, stiletto in hand. The truth can be so told that it becomes the most damaging of lies. It was the way this letter put it that damned Derringforth. The same facts grouped together with kindly shading would not have appeared derogatory to him.

The little Dorothy knew of Derringforth's history agreed perfectly with Varnum's account. The fact that he had told the truth, so far as she could verify his statements, made it evident that the whole letter was truthful. She was forced to regard it as such. With feminine ingenuity, warmed and quickened by love, she conjured up an array of excuses as delicate and sweet as her own nature, that more than overbalanced all but one of Derringforth's shortcomings.

That one was an offense that broke her heart. She could not excuse him for having loved another girl—for loving her even yet, it might be.

Up to this point her justification of him had been complete, but here her reason faltered and she turned away with bitter feelings surging through her soul. Again she was swayed by passion alone, and Derringforth began to look very black. This mood, like the others, ran its course, and as it neared its flood, that love that brought new beauty into the world became deep tinged with hatred for him who inspired it.

The scenes between Derringforth and herself came back to her with realistic vividness. His attitude from the very first had been one calculated to win her love.

"His looks, his words, his soft tones, all show his cruel purpose to amuse himself at my expense, during his enforced imprisonment," she reflected bitterly. She forgot to make allowance for the devotion she had shown him—for the thousand and one little feminine touches—for the smiles and sunshine and merry laughter that would have won the heart of a cynic.

In comparison with Derringforth, Vedder even became the embodiment of virtue. What he had done had been inspired by love.

"There should be some excuse for that," she said. "I am sorry I condemned him so hastily. He was right. It was his duty to let me know—to shield me from such a monster. I should have tried to save him if he had been the one in danger. I never can thank him enough. Why did papa ever bring such a man into his very home? How could he have been so blind? But I was blind until Stanley opened my eyes. I cannot stay in this house with him. He must go. I will never allow myself to see him again. He shall n-e-v-e-r see me again. Oh, it is cruel, cruel!" she moaned, burying her eyes in her hands. " Mama will send him away, and he may be a cripple all his life. I wonder if he didn't really care for me a little! It couldn't have been all pretense—no, no, it could not. I won't believe it of him, I won't think him so wicked, poor fellow. He isn't capable of such cruelty, I know he isn't."

The reaction had come. Love began its sway again. Dorothy's eyes were fixed on Derringforth. The harsh lines of his face became soft, the cruel mockery vanished, the black shadows faded and disappeared, and in their place came an expression of truth—of deep, pure love—the love of a strong, sincere man.

It was when Dorothy had reached this point in her mental tangle that her mother came to her to ask what had happened to Derringforth.

" Oh, Dorothy, my child, you are ill!" exclaimed Mrs. Rayburn in anxious tones, and she ran to her and took her tenderly in her motherly arms.

" My head has ached badly," answered Dorothy, with downcast eyes, " but it is beginning to feel better now. I think it will be all right in a little while," and then she added, with precipitate haste, "Why didn't you tell me last night that you were going away for the day?"

"I didn't decide to go until this morning," explained Mrs. Rayburn.

Dorothy drew a long breath of relief, which was suddenly checked when her mother added, "But it seems that I would better have stayed at home, as I come back to find you in your room ill, and Mr. Derringforth gone mad."

"Gone mad!" repeated Dorothy, springing up with blanched face.

"That is what the doctor says. He is here now. Mr. Derringforth sent for him. I saw the note. Mr. Derringforth wants to go to New York tonight. The doctor says he is crazy."

"Oh, this is dreadful, mama!" exclaimed Dorothy. "Dreadful!" she repeated.

"What could have happened to him?" pursued Mrs. Rayburn. "I thought perhaps you knew. I wonder if I ought not to go down—something has gone wrong—maybe he has had bad news from New York."

"Oh, please go, mama, and see what has happened," pleaded Dorothy with an eloquence that she little realized.

Mrs. Rayburn cast one quick look of inquiry at her daughter. Their eyes met. Dorothy's dropped, and the flush of color that suffused her face revealed the secret.

Mrs. Rayburn hurried from the room, her brain awhirl. This was the first intimation she had had that the relations between Derringforth and Dorothy were anything more than friendly. The discovery almost overwhelmed her. She could not realize it—could not trust herself to speak of it to Dorothy. She must be alone; must think. What should she do; what ought she to do? She was hurrying toward her own room when she heard, spoken in rasping tones, these words: "You might say that you are an ass," and these from Derringforth's lips in reply: "Yes, I might well say it."

She stopped, and with sudden impulse flew to Derringforth's rescue. She had barely entered his presence when she was startled by the apparition of her husband. A minute later, when she found herself in his strong arms, she was convinced that it was no apparition at all.

Colonel Rayburn had come on unannounced on purpose to surprise her. His coming was never more opportune.

"Heaven has sent him," whispered Mrs. Rayburn to herself. "I never needed him so much as now."

It was as Derringforth had feared. The colonel had been sent for, and here he was. Derringforth could not repress a shudder as he steeled himself for the worst. He was in for it, and he would be a man, he said to himself. There was nothing to be ashamed of in loving so sweet a girl. He resolved to defend his position in a dignified way. A rush of thoughts passed through his mind in that one second of silence, and then——

"Phil, my boy, how are you?" came from Colonel Rayburn's lips. "And you, doctor—how are you—and how is your patient coming on?—well, I am sure, since he is in your hands."

"No, no, not at all well," protested the old surgeon.

"What, not doing well—Phil, is this so? Tell me yourself," said the colonel, taking Derringforth's hand in warm greeting.

"I am sorry to contradict so able an authority," replied Derringforth, "but the facts compel me to do so. I am so well that I have been talking to the doctor about going to New York."

"What have you to say for yourself, doctor?" demanded Colonel Rayburn.

"This letter will explain," replied the old surgeon, extending the note from Derringforth. "If it does not convince you of his madness then I will retire from the case."

"There is no doubt of it," returned the colonel, when he had glanced at the note. "What does this mean, Phil? What has happened?"

Derringforth's face showed his embarrassment. There were three pairs of keen eyes upon it, and he could feel that it was ablaze with color. Still he maintained a wonderful coolness, and asked if it wasn't natural that he should be anxious to get back to New York and begin straightening out his business. This did very well as a bluff, but it did not mislead Colonel Rayburn. He said nothing more, however, just then, preferring to look about a little, thinking he might discover the cause for himself.

"Now that Mr. Rayburn is here I think we can manage to keep Mr. Derringforth," said Mrs. Rayburn to the doctor. When the latter was gone she drew her husband aside and told him of her discovery.

"H'm, h'm," said the colonel, undisturbed by the revelation, "that explains Phil's anxiety to get away. But I can't understand how it has come about. What has become of Stanley?"

"You take it very coolly, dear," protested Mrs. Rayburn, made doubly nervous by her husband's philosophic manner.

"Yes, why not? It will work out all right. Don't say a word to either of them—don't let them know that we know. They are in love; they have had a misunderstanding. It's a bad combination to mix up in, my dear—we will keep out."

And they kept out, but their eyes were very wide open. It was an interesting problem—in some respects a painful one. Derringforth had a firm champion in the colonel. Mrs. Rayburn liked him. She was becoming very fond of him before she discovered his purpose to take her daughter from her. She was not one of those foolish mothers who think their daughters should not marry until their youth and sweetness have vanished. The thought of losing Dorothy, nevertheless, was a bitter one to her.

When Dorothy learned of Derringforth's desire to leave the house, of his own free will, without being invited to go—forced to go, if you please—it lent a different complexion to the matter. It began to look as if he were anticipating the Rayburn move, and was ready to "go them one better." This took away all the glory of sending him off. It began to dawn on her that it did not show good judgment to act too hastily. There was a possibility of making a mistake, and Derringforth was one with whom she wished to avoid anything of this sort.

She looked in the mirror. Horrors! How her eyes were swollen, how wan she looked! No, no, she could not see him then—she would not have him see her for the world. She rang for a servant.

"Tell Mr. Derringforth," she said, "that my head is bothering me a good deal today, and that I may not get in to see him before morning."

"That ought to bridge matters a little," she told herself when the servant had gone. "It will give me time to think, and time to make myself look a little more like myself. If not, I hope he will never see me—he would be horrified—ooh!"

Dorothy's message pacified Derringforth slightly, but it seemed to him like a compromise measure—

like the result of urging on the part of some one—
most likely Colonel Rayburn—in the interest of harmony. He was accordingly on the ice bound shores
of dignity when Dorothy called in the morning. She
didn't quite know whether to open her heart and
forgive him for all the offenses he might have been
guilty of, or to be diplomatically courteous, freez-
ingly reserved. She knew one thing, and that was
that she loved him—loved him enough to fall down
on her knees and worship him, but there was that
other girl, and there was a proper regard for self
respect to be kept in mind.

At best, then, she must act a part, and she acted it
very crudely. Derringforth felt his heart freeze, and
the atmosphere from that region chilled his expression, so that Dorothy shuddered as if pierced by a
northeast blast in mid winter. She hurried from the
room, making a palpably awkward excuse to get away.
Then a little crying and a little hating in turn, and
she was generally wretched. These moods were overcome by the tender passion now and again, and so
the day went by with her and she did not see Derringforth until evening. She had vowed that she
would not see him then; that she did not know when
she would see him—perhaps not for several days. But
her vows melted as such vows do when they come in
touch with love ablaze.

Derringforth felt more like getting away now than
ever, but Colonel Rayburn's presence kept him quiet

so far as outward evidences of his desire went. Dorothy's face was warmer when she came in in the evening to bring him the mail. If his had been equally warm, the ice between them would have melted like magic, and there would have been a rejoicing of two hearts that would have reached to heaven and made the immortals smile. But Derringforth was not in the mood to enliven the heavenly abode with anything that would speed a wave of approval through that region.

Dorothy was more patient than in the morning, and less susceptible to the reflection of his discomfiture. But he could not throw off the depression speedily enough to save her from taking on something of his mood, and then all progress towards a better understanding was checked in each.

It was a chilling atmosphere for Dorothy's young love. Derringforth thought till his brain whirled, trying to diagnose the situation. It appeared to him somewhat cloudy in spots. He could not quite make Dorothy out.

"If I offended her, and I must have done so," he argued, "why does she come in to see me at all? I shouldn't think she would. On the other hand, if she was not offended at what I did, what has happened? She is changed. There is a continent between us, and there is a cold winter settling down over that continent. I wish I were somewhere else, but I'm here—very much here, and—I might as well say it, it's no use to try to humbug myself—I'm here and in love with the girl that freezes me into an ice cake—freezes me so solid that I can't think straight, can't wink straight, can't do anything but lie here and wait for the crash. Something has got to happen; the tension is too great."

But nothing did happen. It would have been better if there had. An explosion is sometimes a good thing. It does away with a world of anxiety, clears the atmosphere, and lets in the sunlight. This is what an explanation does, but an explanation in such cases is hard to get at without the explosion, and too many times there is no flash to set off the upheaval.

So it went on, and Derringforth and Dorothy got no nearer to each other than the lines of studied politeness. But the fires of love so recently kindled in their hearts still burned dimly in the heavy atmosphere, in which flame flickered feebly and blue.

At last Derringforth was able to leave his bed. He made preparations for an early start for New York. When the time came to say good by, then it was that the hearts of these two threw off the disguise. It was a tender parting, but withal discreet. Derringforth went away very happy, while Dorothy began to realize the depth of her love for him. How empty and lonely the house without him!

But between him and herself there was still the image of her of whom Varnum wrote. Who was she?

Dorothy had asked herself this question vaguely one or two thousand times, but now she asked it earnestly —asked it as one who intends to hunt down the information she seeks, be it near or far, be it on the highway of easy access, or in the jungle where danger threatens with menacing finger.

XLVIII.

It was mid winter. The night air was crisp and sharp. A million pairs of metropolitan eyes were already closed in slumber. The toilers of the big city were being refreshed for the coming day. The side streets, except for the occasional appearance of a night owl straggling homeward, were deserted. Stretching away from a Fifth Avenue palace was a long line of carriages. As fast as the occupants of one of these alighted, and disappeared under the awning leading to the entrance, another carriage took its place, and the line in the rear was constantly reinforced by fresh arrivals.

Marion Kingsley, accompanied by her father and mother, tripped lightly up the carpeted steps to the brilliantly lighted mansion.

The Kingsleys were followed by a little old man, very thin and very feeble. Leaning on his arm was his young wife, a girl in the bloom of health, and beaming with love for her antique partner, whose purse was big with yellow coin.

The next was a well mated couple—a man and wife

with refined, happy faces. A glance was enough to convince one that the world had gone well with them —that each had been to the other an inspiration, a joy, a happiness that is God's best gift to the earthly life.

A solitary figure followed them up the steps—an old man with sloping shoulders, slightly bent. He was tall and angular, with very long nose, somewhat thin and inclined toward the Roman type. His eyes were small and rather close together. There was no warmth in them, but they were wonderfully keen, though they had seen many winters. His step had lost its elasticity, and yet it by no means lacked decision. His face showed the wear of time. It showed more than this ; it told the story of a selfish life. He had lived only for himself, and now he was old and alone, with no one to care for him ; with no faculty to care for another. His name was Van Stump. He vanished within the door.

A man, the counterpart of a rich bank president, if not himself such, sprang from his carriage with youthful step, and with the grace of good breeding helped his wife to alight, and then his two daughters. They were sweet, pretty girls, and the soft, warm wraps they wore became them well. It was evident that the father was very proud of them. Happiness beamed from his face as, beside his wife, he led the way up the steps. He had something to show for his life—something to keep it fragrant and in tune with the world. Van Stump had nothing. The contrast between his own and a well ordered life—a well lived life—was conspicuous, sandwiched in as he was between two such happy families.

The occupants of a dozen carriages had vanished within the great doors when two young men passed under the awning and walked gayly up the steps. One of them belonged to the smart set. He was Minton Varnum, and he had brought with him his friend Vedder.

Not long after their arrival a man of fine military presence, accompanied by his wife and daughter, entered the mansion with proud step. It was Colonel Rayburn. The faces of Mrs. Rayburn and Dorothy were bright with expectancy. The Rayburns were a strikingly handsome family.

The next to arrive, of those who have figured in this story, was a young man of fine presence. He had almost decided to send his regrets tonight. "It will be a great crush," he told himself. "And I am utterly worn out from dissipation already," he went on with indecision. "There is only one thing makes me think of going," he continued, yielding. "If she were not to be there no one could tempt me, but ——" Here he stopped suddenly and began to dress for the ball.

This was not Derringforth; it was Burton Edwards. Marion still possessed the magic influence that made him her slave, though it should be said to her credit that she never wilfully misled him—never took advantage of the power she had over him. Her feeling for him was one of pure, simple friendship. She had undertaken what millions of girls have attempted before her, only to fail flatly—a little drama in which a young woman and a young man are to act the part of friends—to be friends, jolly good friends; such friends as boys are to each other, as girls are to each other —chums. The success of her venture was as yet undetermined. Viewed as she viewed it it was full of promise. Viewed with the eyes of the student of human nature, it would have called forth an ominous shake of the head.

Edwards hurriedly left his coat and hat, and went directly to the ball room to find Marion. He found her. She was in animated conversation with Richard Devonshire. The sight stunned him. He would have turned back and escaped from the house, but Marion saw him—saw that he was coming to her. There was then but one thing for him to do. He must join her and Devonshire, and look pleased—must take the hand of the latter and express delight at seeing him again.

This was no easy thing to do. His nature rebelled against it, but he was well versed in the conventionalities of polite society, and knew that its canons must not be outraged. His words of greeting to Devonshire were rather warm than otherwise. In acting a part it is difficult to command the proper tones and expressions. Beyond an unnatural paleness there was nothing in his looks to reveal his true feelings.

"Isn't this the most delightful surprise, Burton?" said Marion, her eyes sparkling, and then looking into Devonshire's face she added, "Why didn't you let us know of the pleasure in store for us?"

"So that you could have enjoyed it in anticipation, eh?" returned Devonshire.

"Yes, certainly, I think you were very selfish."

"I'm afraid I was. You see I wished you to be glad to see me, and feared that if you had had a week's association with me in anticipation you would already have become weary of me."

"Isn't that mean, Burton? Did you ever hear anything like it?" protested Marion.

Edwards was again called upon to smile and confirm Marion's views, though he would have liked to say, as he expressed it in his own mind, that Devonshire was dead right in his conclusions. It required no little restraint to keep from putting this thought into words.

As soon as he could do so without too great abruptness, he made an excuse to get away. The strain on him was too much. He wanted to be alone—to be anywhere but in Devonshire's presence. So he felt then, but he had no sooner got away than he wished he had remained where he was. He began to realize that he had yielded the field to Devonshire without a struggle.

He passed from the ball room out into the main parlor. The room was packed with people. He stopped to speak to a friend. After the exchange of a few words he turned to pass on toward the door. As he did so he came face to face with Derringforth.

The latter had just arrived. It was the first time these two men had met since that first meeting in Marion's home. Each recognized the other instantly; each felt a sinking sensation at the heart; each was like marble. There was an instant's pause, and then their hands met. They were gentlemen. It was a bitter moment for Derringforth. The past rushed back over him with a force that was almost overwhelming.

"It has been a long time since we have met, Mr. Edwards," he said, speaking with an effort. His voice was wavering.

"Yes," returned Edwards; "it has been a long time. I hope you are well."

His words did not flow easily. There was a restraint in his manner that was wholly unlike his generous, free nature.

A few more sentences and they parted. Edwards went up stairs, and, putting on his coat and hat, went out into the cold night air, and wandered aimlessly from street to street. The stars looked down upon him, and with twinkling eyes smiled at his folly.

His few words with Derringforth did Edwards good. He had touched hands with one whose sufferings had been keener than his own. He saw it all at a glance, and his pity went out to Derringforth. The manly greeting of the latter—the impress of his hand—carried force. Edwards felt this—felt himself irresistibly drawn to the man he had most feared.

Derringforth likewise understood Edwards. That one moment's conversation established a silent bond of sympathy between them. But to forgive Edwards—to forget—would have required the charity of a god.

"It was he who first broke in upon my happiness," sighed Derringforth, with a sadness as of death; "he who first taught her to love another than myself. No man has ever dealt me a blow so cruel; no man ever can. The first stab hurts most. It was a revelation worse than death—worse than all the other tortures of life piled high one above another. One experience such as this is all God permits man to suffer. There may be repetitions, but they are not the same."

A wave of music from the orchestra flooded the ball room, bursting through the door and rolling on from room to room. The dancers sprang to their feet and plunged into the waltz with merry hearts.

Derringforth worked his way forward till at length his eyes were within range of the whirling, seething sea of terpsichorean devotees. Never had he beheld a scene more beautiful, more inspiring. The room itself was an ideal conception. Its decoration was unique, bordering on the æsthetic. The lighting was the latest expression of art. It was plentiful but soft —that sort of light in which beauty is most beautiful.

The smart set of the metropolis was there; youth with the gay world just burst upon its vision was there; middle age that had drunk deep of these pleasures was there; and old age was there—old age whose enjoyment was flashed over memory's lines, the scenes of youth brought back by the scene before it.

Derringforth had reached the door. He looked at the beauty of the room, and the beauty on the floor. Graceful girls with bright faces, and men of faultless bearing, whirled toward him and vanished. The music was an inspiration. He felt it tingle along his nerves. He had not seen Dorothy yet. It was she who brought him there. But there was another whom he longed to see; whom he dreaded to see.

"If I could only see her and she not see me," he said to himself, looking thoughtfully toward the floor.

He raised his eyes; they met Marion's. There was a flash of recognition, and she was gone. But in that one instant he saw in her face enough to set his brain on fire. He dare not remain where he was; he dare not go to Dorothy just now. He worked his way back through the door, and, moving to one side, where he could not be seen from the ball room, leaned against the wall for support.

The picture of Marion's face was before him. He held it up and began studying it. It was full of meaning. Tenderness, doubt, hope, gladness, surprise, forgiveness, regret—these were all there, but chief among them was gladness—gladness so fine, so tender, that Derringforth's heart melted. Two people were never more unlike than Marion herself, and the distorted likeness of her—the creation of his imagination. He held them side by side in wonder, in regret, in humiliation.

Marion had come to the ball in the best of spirits. A long walk in the cold, crisp air, that afternoon, had proved a tonic that sent the color to her cheeks and the tingle of abounding health through her frame. All this was supplemented by her surprise and delight at seeing Devonshire. In a way, she was very fond of him. He was another with whom she had undertaken to enact the same rôle that she was playing with Burton Edwards. She had not yet made a success with either of them; she had not yet made a failure.

In a Parisian gown that was the embodiment of art and the envy of every other woman, Marion was at her best. She had never looked sweeter; had never talked better. To Devonshire she was the only girl in the ball room. It was with him she was dancing when her eyes met Derringforth's.

She reeled in Devonshire's arms. Her face was deathly pale. He supported her to a seat, frightened and anxious.

"I shall be all right in a few minutes," she said. "I must have been a little faint. I am already feeling better."

"Shall I not get you a glass of water?" asked Devonshire, feeling that he must do something.

"No, oh no, please don't—don't do anything to attract attention. No one realized why we left the floor, I hope."

"No, I think not. I was careful to avoid that."

"I am so glad—what a foolish thing for me to do! I am feeling very well now — am I not looking better? I feel the blood coming into my cheeks again—they are beginning to burn—it was such a sudden freak—I hope you will pardon me for giving you this fright—I never did such an inane thing before."

Marion hardly knew what she was saying. Her brain was spinning madly. The shock for the moment had nearly upset her reason. "Phil!" she cried to herself when she saw him. This one word, and her heart gave a great bound of gladness, and for an instant everything was blank. She kept on with her partner mechanically, and then somehow she found herself in a chair. It was all the work of a second, but to her it seemed the duration of a lifetime.

There was one who saw the color fade from Marion's face. It was Dorothy. She too left the floor, scarcely less precipitately and with no more color.

Marion knew nothing of Dorothy; Dorothy knew everything of Marion. The Rayburns spent their winters in New York, and were society people.

Marion had met Colonel and Mrs. Rayburn—had in fact been entertained by them, but Dorothy was a school girl then. Marion had been in Europe two years ; Dorothy had come out during her absence.

Most obstacles melt when the concentrated rays of earnestness are brought to bear upon them. Dorothy found this out when she began, as she should have begun at first, in a rational way to discover the identity of her whom Burrock accredited with turning Derringforth's head. She had a very clear conception of " that designing creature," as she sometimes mentally styled her—a conception that was the product of jealousy. It is needless to say that this picture was unlike Marion ; it is needless to describe it beyond hinting at its cruel, cunning, cold expression, beneath which a satanic spirit lurked—so very satanic, in fact, that Dorothy shuddered and shut her eyes in fear whenever she beheld it.

Marion's beauty and popularity were familiar to Dorothy. She had read of her in the society columns ; had heard her mother speak of her in warm praise, and once she had seen in a metropolitan paper, more pretentious in the matter of art than the daily, a portrait of Marion. It was a tolerably truthful likeness, and being such must have of necessity been very pretty —Dorothy thought it wonderfully pretty. Her surprise, then, when she learned that Marion, and her own conception of the woman who had played such havoc with Derringforth, were one and the same, was absolutely painful, if surprise ever reaches that point. At all events Dorothy was so disconcerted that she wasn't quite sure whether she was in her right mind or not. She declared that she would never construct any more pictures, and with deep chagrin looked down upon her imagination with bitter contempt, vowing that it was not in keeping with the other faculties of a girl of ordinary intelligence, which she hoped she was; but even this hope sloped toward the realm of doubt.

This was Dorothy's feeling then, and her vow was natural. But a girl can no more keep her imagination in check than she can force back with her delicate hand the tides of the great ocean. This is pretty true of humanity in general, but it may be a little truer of girls than of any one else.

Dorothy was terribly "cut up" over this matter. She felt that she owed Marion an apology. If she had been anybody in this world other than the one Derringforth had loved—loved even now, perhaps—she would certainly have apologized. But there are points at which humanity, be it ever so refined, draws the line. Apologizing to Marion was one of these points with Dorothy.

"I don't care if I do feel mean about it," she said to herself. "I simply won't, and that is all there is about it. I won't, won't, won't!" And metaphorically she stamped her pretty little foot to emphasize her refusal to do the thing she felt she ought to do.

XLIX.

It seemed to Burton Edwards that he had walked over half of New York. He had in fact walked over very little of it. Not that his step was at all sluggish. On the contrary, it was feverish in the extreme. The simple truth was that he had been out only a few minutes when he returned to the scene of gayety, but to him these minutes were hours, for Devonshire was with Marion.

Edwards reëntered the ball room very soon after Derringforth so suddenly left it, and before Marion had had time to regain control of herself. He saw the anxious look on Devonshire's face, and noted with alarm Marion's strange manner and pale features.

"Devonshire has done it," he said to himself, casting a withering look at the Englishman, which fortunately was not seen. "Confound him! I'd like to throttle him," he went on. "What is he over here for, any way, and just as it was beginning to be clear sailing for me? I'm getting tired of my luck. I'm getting tired of everything. I wish I had stayed at home;

then I should not have been disturbed by this fellow's presence—not tonight, any way. It's fate, that is what it is. Something always happens just at the wrong time."

Marion turned her head anxiously toward the orchestra, saying to herself, "Oh, if it would only begin playing!" And as if in response to her wish it did begin. "Thank heaven," said Marion beneath her breath. "I would rather fall on the floor than have these two men look at me as they do." And then, turning toward Edwards, she said, "Come, Burton, let us try the polka—Mr. Devonshire will excuse us for a minute or two, I am sure."

Edwards was only too ready to comply with her suggestion, and there was perhaps a gleam of triumph in his eyes as he beheld the look of astonishment and dismay that flashed to Devonshire's face.

When the strains of music ceased Derringforth came back into the ball room, having steadied his nerves in quiet meditation. He saw Dorothy about two thirds of the way down the room. Beside her was a young man whose manner indicated that he was drawing heavily upon his reserve resources to make himself especially "fetching." This young man was Mr. Stanley Vedder.

Derringforth disliked to interrupt a *tête à tête*, but this had the appearance of being a lopsided one, as Dorothy did not respond with equal warmth to the exuberance of her companion. This was evident at a distance.

Derringforth, emboldened by this phase of the situation, and by the further fact that Dorothy must have been expecting him for at least half an hour, walked with easy stride to join them.

"Well, I'm here, Dorothy," he said cheerfully; "a little late, but I have kept my promise, you see—hope you are having a good time," and turning to Vedder and extending his hand added, "this is indeed a surprise. I am glad to see you—have you been in town long?"

His hand was not taken. Vedder refused to recognize him. It was a deliberate cut, and before many eyes—one pair in particular that flashed fire as they beheld the affront.

Derringforth was astounded at Vedder's extraordinary action. Dorothy was scarcely less surprised. She had not forgotten the Varnum letter, but there was nothing in that even to suggest that Vedder would dare insult a friend of hers in her presence, and in such a place. She was well aware of his jealousy, but she had always regarded him as a gentleman.

Derringforth knew nothing of his bitter enmity. The discovery of it came as a blow between the eyes. It dazed him for a second. It was too much to realize on the instant that one who had enjoyed Dorothy's friendship could so far forget himself.

Marion could scarcely restrain herself from flying to Derringforth's aid. It was a moment of supreme suspense with her. Would he be able to control himself, or would outraged manhood strike back and hurl the insolent cad to the floor?

Dorothy's face was flushed with indignation and shame; Derringforth's was very white. Beyond this he showed no sign of the volcanic fires within him.

Outwardly he was the coolest man in the room. The dignity with which he bore the insult was a revelation to Marion. As the truth broke upon him he seemed to become suddenly taller and broader. The pose of his head, and his whole attitude, bespoke the man of quality and power. With one withering look of contempt flashed down at Vedder, he turned to Dorothy and said:

"Shall we not join your father and mother? I have not seen them yet." There was no emotion in his voice—nothing to indicate the depth of his feeling. He had himself under perfect control.

"Yes, oh, yes," answered Dorothy. There was almost a pathetic pleading in her tones.

Vedder's face blazed with anger and chagrin. His plan to humiliate Derringforth had resulted in his own humiliation. Dorothy had deserted him, and he was disgraced. A hundred eyes were upon him. His expression was pitiable as he stood there alone, enraged and ashamed. He shot a quick, appealing glance about him for some means of escape. Varnum was coming toward him.

A few minutes later these two and another could have been seen together in a far corner of the hall, talking with much earnestness and frequent and emphatic gesticulation. Van Stump was the third member of the trio. He had seen the bitter contempt flashed from Derringforth's eyes, and had seen him walk away in triumph. He had already learned to his sorrow a good deal of Derringforth's forceful qualities; he had a better idea of them now. With his hatred for his old enemy he was scarcely less enraged than Vedder himself, and at once decided to go to the latter and offer to help him to bring Derringforth's haughty head to the dust.

"I have crushed him once and I will do it again," said Van Stump, with malicious fire in his little, deep set eyes.

There was something in Dorothy's touch as she took his arm, something in the expression of her face as she looked up into his, that made Derringforth's heart bound. For the moment Vedder was forgotten; for the moment all indignation was forgotten. The distance between him and Dorothy had vanished. There were many eyes that followed him with wonder as the two walked down the room—eyes that had witnessed the humiliating affront to which he had been subjected, and now marveled at the coolness of his manner, and at the smile that lighted up his face.

But there was one who read him better—who interpreted better. That one was Marion. Love quickens the faculties; lends keenness to intuition. It was a cruel revelation. The worst stab Derringforth had ever received had not been more cruel than this one was to Marion. It had come to her with a suddenness that gave intensity to the sting. She had had no preparation; no suspicion of the horrible truth that now broke upon her. Phil in love with another girl—no, no, it could not be, it must not be! Phil, the delight of her youth—the old and only love of her life!

She had not thought of caring for any one else as she cared for him; she never could care for any one else as she cared for him. Other men entertained her and amused her. There was a kind of delight— a kind of intoxication in all this that tickled the palate of an artificial taste. But in it all there was nothing restful, nothing sustaining, nothing satisfying. The wooing of Edwards and Devonshire and her many other admirers had not dislodged—had in no wise disturbed—that deep abiding love of her heart which began away back in the early days of childhood.

She was not alone responsible for the estrangement between Derringforth and herself. He had contributed quite as largely toward it as she. Neither had done anything intentionally to widen the gap that now separated them. A false theory—a wrong start—and all else had come of itself. With insidious tread distance crept in between them and forced them further and further apart.

It is saddening to note how the gap between two

souls widens when once a break has come. The merest little nothings become mountains from which cold, wintry blasts sweep down to chill the heart into unyielding ice. One moment of frank talk, freed from petty pride, and all coldness would melt into summer sunshine. Oh, that Marion and Derringforth had had such a talk! The wrong start would have been righted, and their lives would have flowed on together in perfect confidence, in perfect harmony; such harmony and joy as come only to them whose lives God has willed shall be made one.

But malicious fate, with cunning hand, interposed conditions between Marion and Phil that neither had the bigness of soul to surmount; and so each drifted further and further from the other as time sped on.

Marion had thought, as people are wont to think —as the feminine mind especially is wont to think— that somehow, some way, the coldness between Phil and herself would be dissipated, and then the old happy days would return and Phil and she would be to each other as they once had been—each loving the other with the same sweet, simple, trustful love that made their early lives so bright.

But the last three years had been her play day— her long vacation before settling down to the serious side of life. When this play day was over, she had often said to herself, she would then make Phil the happiest boy in the world. She would love him as no other man was ever loved. She would give him all her devotion, all her thought, all her life. This was something to look forward to—something she had looked forward to, and it had given her many happy hours that would otherwise have been tinged in somber hue.

All this was very real to her. She expected it as a matter of course, almost as a matter of right, as an only child expects to inherit his father's property. The thought that Phil loved the girl beside him was so severe a shock to Marion that it shook the foundations of her life. She felt as if death itself had pierced her heart. Until now she had never known keenest torture; until now she had never known how deeply she loved Derringforth; until now she had never known what jealousy was.

Burton Edwards saw Derringforth when he entered the room. He watched him with breathless interest as he walked toward Dorothy and Vedder. He saw the affront, and felt his blood tingle with indignation —felt it tingle, too, with admiration for Derringforth, as he saw him walk away in triumph with the sweet girl beside him.

"Did you ever see anything so cool?" he exclaimed. "Did you ever see any one so completely squelched? Who is this miserable cad, I wonder? And the girl—isn't she pretty? See, see the way she looks up into his face, by Jove!" And with this final exclamation, into which his whole vocabulary of admiration was compressed, he turned to Marion for confirmation. One quick glance, and he drew himself back, thoroughly frightened. Marion was like death.

"I am a little faint," she said, seeing his alarm and forcing herself to speak.

"You are very pale—you are seriously ill—what shall I do?" said Edwards nervously.

"I shall be all right in a few minutes," returned Marion.

"Shall I not bring your mother?"

"No, it would do no good. I will go with you to her after a little while."

When the first force of the shock was over, Marion looked less ghastly, but there was no life in her face; no light in her eyes. She tried to talk, hoping to hide the secret that was killing her, but she did not succeed. Edwards, blind as he was in matters of love, could not shut his eyes to anything so plain.

"She loves him," he groaned almost audibly. His face told the keenness of his suffering. Marion understood him, and pitied him with all her own aching heart. She knew how to pity now, but she was powerless to give him the comfort he craved. Love is not a puppet of the mind to be placed here and there at will. It does its own thinking; forms its own ties.

Derringforth and Dorothy had been with Colonel and Mrs. Rayburn but a few minutes when the orchestra brought the dancing men suddenly to their feet and sent them scurrying about for their partners. A dapper young man of the bandbox order hurried toward Dorothy. She saw him coming, and exclaimed impulsively: "Oh, I can't dance with him this time."

"With whom?" asked Mrs. Rayburn, somewhat surprised.

"Mr. Grammasy — see, here he comes. What shall I tell him?—oh, quick, mama!"

"But Dorothy, my dear, you would not break an engagement, I am sure, unless there is some very good excuse."

Dorothy looked up appealingly to Derringforth.

"I wish I could suggest something to save you," he said quickly, "but Mr. Grammasy will be offended."

Dorothy's heart sank. Mr. Grammasy presented himself with one of those regulation smiles of the effusive order that very young men and some very silly old men are wont to employ on such occasions. "I believe I am to have the pleasure——"

"Yes," answered Dorothy in a way that did credit to her regard for conventionality; and in another minute her feet were keeping time to the music.

Derringforth watched her with admiring eyes until she was lost among the dancers. Then, in turning toward Mrs. Rayburn, he saw Marion at some distance down the room. He wondered that she was not dancing. Her eyes were fixed upon the floor.

"This is not like Marion," he said to himself.

Mrs. Rayburn talked on lightly. Derringforth answered mechanically, and seemed to be listening to her words while he heard nothing. Presently Marion looked up and turned her eyes toward him. He was not near enough to read their expression, but there was something so pathetic in her manner that he felt impelled to go to her. Acting on this impulse he asked Mrs. Rayburn to excuse him, saying he wished to speak to a friend.

Marion saw him get up and after a moment's conversation turn and walk toward her. Was he coming to her—Phil actually coming to her? Her heart throbbed wildly, sending a flood of color into her pale cheeks. Derringforth was scarcely less moved. The strong emotions that swayed him almost overcame his self possession.

Marion could feel his approach, and a thousand fancies surged hotly through her brain. It was an instant of expectancy and dread—a moment of awful suspense—when the sweet sound of Derringforth's voice broke upon her ears. One word—"Marion!" he uttered in trembling tones. She looked up quickly, timidly. Her eyes filled with tears that burst forth from the deep, secret chambers of her heart. He held out his hand; she gave him hers. Neither spoke for a minute save by the silent touch of palm to palm; and in that communion was felt the thrill that awakened memories dearer than life itself.

Burton Edwards needed no more ; he could endure no more. With emotion that rent his soul, and with magnanimity that was almost divine, he clasped Derringforth's hand, and with warm grasp and delightful courtesy bade him take his place beside Marion. Then, turning to her, he excused himself with delicate consideration for her feelings, and hurriedly left the room.

Derringforth, having thanked Edwards, sat down beside Marion for the first time since the night of that memorable interview, now more than two years ago.

Fate, that ever vigilant being whose eagle eye sees deep into the secret recesses of the soul, was prepared, as usual, to turn this meeting to good account. Burton Edwards might have been at the other side of the room ; so might Dorothy. Then both would have been spared the tortures that tore deep furrows into their hearts. But fate willed differently. Dorothy saw the meeting, and knew the cause of the emotion that swayed Phil and Marion. She saw Burton Edwards leave the room with drooping shoulders and bowed head.

"I am glad you have come to me, Phil. I have wanted to see you so much."

Marion spoke these words with a deep feeling that penetrated straight to Derringforth's heart. There was that in her manner and in the soft light of her eyes which made him see clearly through his false conception of her, and brought him once more face to face with the sweet girl of his youth—the Marion Kingsley as she was in very truth.

Derringforth said nothing for a moment. His soul was too full to speak. He looked at the dancers with vacant stare, and thought. His fingers fumbled nervously at an imaginary watch chain. Dorothy passed close to him. He looked straight into her eyes, but did not see her. Then he turned to Marion, and with an emotion that almost precluded speech, said:

"Marion, I have been unjust to you. You have convinced me in these two or three words that I have not understood you."

"Did you think I would not care to see you?" asked Marion with trembling lips.

"I did not know what else to think," Phil said slowly.

"And yet you came to me with this feeling?"

"I could not help coming to you. There was something in the way you looked toward me that appealed to me with resistless force."

There was a moment's silence and then Marion said,

"Yes, Phil, you have been unjust to me—oh, how unjust!"

The words were spoken tenderly, sorrowfully. They cut deep.

"I do not know how to answer you, Marion. I wish I could have learned the truth before."

Marion looked up quickly, a horrible fear blanching her face. She could not speak. Derringforth paused. The silence that ensued was unbearable.

"Do you know how long it has been, Marion, since we have seen each other?" he went on with downcast eyes. "You know," he continued without waiting for a reply, "you must know something of the sorrows that have come into my life during this time."

His words trembled on his lips. The thought of his father and mother, added to the other emotions that stirred him at this moment, choked back his faltering speech.

"Yes, Phil, I understand, and I am so sorry for you. I wanted, oh, how much I wanted to go to you and tell you how deeply I sympathized with you, though it was not till I returned home from Europe a few weeks ago that I learned of your affliction."

"Not until a few weeks ago?" exclaimed Derringforth, astounded.

"No, not until then. We were nearing Sandy Hook. Papa bought a paper from the pilot. There was an article in it in which the death of both your father and mother was incidentally mentioned. I was never so surprised. I could hardly bring myself to believe it true. It was too much to realize. I cannot thoroughly realize it even yet."

Derringforth looked at Marion in amazement. "It is almost beyond my comprehension," he said.

"Oh, Phil, this is cruel! How could you think so badly of me—think me so indifferent as to learn of your father's death, and then of your mother's, and never write you one word of sympathy?"

"The thought was forced upon me," responded Derringforth. "Think for a minute; recount the circumstances—all the circumstances, and tell me if I could have come to any other conclusion."

"There is an intelligence that sees deeper than the brain," answered Marion. "Those who have known each other as we have should not let circumstantial evidence drive them to a hasty judgment. Did not intuition, even in spite of logic, teach you a truer opinion of me?"

"There can be but one answer to that, and yet the facts, as I saw them, were arrayed in such force against this opinion—this feeling, that gradually I became convinced you had severed forever all the ties between us. At times I was impelled to write you, and almost yielded, but I could not bring myself to forget. I could not believe that one who had been so close to me as you had would, if the slightest spark of interest in me remained, go off to Europe for a prolonged stay without so much as informing me of her departure—much less saying good by to me. You remember the circumstances of our last meeting. You cannot have forgotten the purpose of that meeting. All this was fresh in your mind a week or so later, when you sailed for Europe. You must have known the disappointment I felt. Your heart—that deeper intelligence to which you refer—could not have been blind. Think for one minute, Marion, and tell me if I was wrong—tell me if under these circumstances I could have written to you?"

Derringforth's voice had gained in intensity of feeling as he went on—as the pent up grievance of his soul for the first time took form in words. This emotion—this quiet, passionate utterance—was a pathetic appeal that rent Marion's heart and disclosed in a single stroke the cause of the rift between them that had gradually widened into a chasm.

"Phil," she exclaimed, unconsciously raising her hand in protest, and with a look of pained astonishment so deep that in that one word—in that look—was revealed to him a truth that was no less astounding to Derringforth than were his words to her.

An explanation that would have given each a clear insight into the heart of the other was imminent. But the word had scarcely died away on Marion's lips when Devonshire walked quickly across the room and joined them.

If guided by the hand of his satanic majesty, the Englishman could not have swept down upon Derringforth and Marion at a more critical moment. The light was breaking upon their vision. They were just beginning to see through the mist that had for many weary months obscured the true impulses of each other's heart. The mutual misunderstanding that had turned the sunshine of their lives into darkness was about to be cleared away.

But not yet. Fate willed otherwise, and Devonshire, obedient to the touch of this imperious hand from the realm of shadow, came suddenly upon them; chilling as by a blast from the frozen North the budding hopes of reconciliation. Marion's whole soul rebelled at this interruption, and cried out in bitter protest. It required all the sweetness of her nature, all the tact of a clever girl, to disguise her feelings and welcome Devonshire as his position and friendly relations with her demanded. She smiled pleasantly and with throbbing heart presented him to Derringforth.

It was the first time these two men had ever met. The eyes of each flashed a quick look at the other, and an icy atmosphere swept suddenly over the trio. Derringforth! Devonshire! In the other's name each recognized one who had stood between him and Marion—between him and that rounder, fuller happiness that could be had only by winning her to be his wife.

Neither Derringforth nor Devonshire could wholly disguise his feelings. Both were too well bred to be rude; both struggled to avoid the cold tones that made their utterances cut like the breath of winter.

Marion spoke softly, and, looking up into Devonshire's face with a smile designed to soothe the harshness of his impulse, said: "Mr. Derringforth and I are very old friends—you have heard me speak of him, I am sure. We were children together.'

Mr. Derringforth! Phil shuddered. How formal —how cold and distant these words from Marion's lips, which had never before, in his presence, called him anything but Phil. And the light of her eyes, and the soft, almost delighted tones of her voice—at what discord with his own bitter feelings!

There stood the man before him who had perhaps done more than any other to turn the bright sunshine of his youth into shadow. To take his hand as Derringforth had taken it was a miserable mockery. He almost loathed himself. And yet Marion could welcome Devonshire with a gracious smile—this man who had helped to rob him of what had been the dearest treasure of life.

"I may see you again before the evening is over," he said to Marion, rising abruptly. His words were spoken hastily and without thought. Then, turning to Devonshire, he added, "Will you be in New York for some time? I am sure you will find it very gay here at present."

In these words to Devonshire he avoided the sin of hypocrisy that he so much detested. He was gone almost before either Marion or Devonshire had time to reply.

It was a struggle for Marion to keep back the tears. Devonshire saw the color vanish from her face, and now he knew the cause of the sudden shock that had almost overcome her earlier in the evening. His own heart was like lead. The mystery was solved.

At last it was clear why he could never get closer to her than the lines of friendship. He had known all along that Burton Edwards was not the man that stood between them. He had no fear of him.

Marion's eyes followed Derringforth until he had almost reached Dorothy, and then with a visible shudder she turned suddenly away.

"I may see you again before the evening is over." She repeated the words to herself. They cut like a keen blade. There was something, too, in Derringforth's manner as he uttered them that froze her very soul.

"He does not understand me," she cried mentally. "He will not understand me. Oh, this bitter fate!"

L.

A PROCESSION of heavily laden market wagons was making its way slowly down Fifth Avenue. The crunching and grinding of the cold steel tires upon the frosty pavement reached the delicate ears of a young woman, and sent a chill scurrying along her nerves. She looked out of the window of her carriage and up into the faces of the stolid market men, muffled almost to their eyes.

"What a life!" she thought. "These poor fellows must have been up all night to get here at this unearthly hour. I pity them. The world can't seem very bright to their eyes. What a lot of hardships and disappointments and sorrows there are in life!"

She was in the mood that sees only the somber side. A few minutes later she had reached home. She went direct to her room, followed by her maid.

"I am sorry you remained up for me, Mary," she said, in tones of genuine regret. "I shall not need you—it is too bad."

The great clock below stairs struck three times. Marion hurriedly closed the door as if to shut out the dread sound. She threw off her wraps, and went quickly to her writing desk and took out a photograph. It was one that for three years had stood before her every time she sat down to write. She held it up so that a good light was on it, and after looking at it for a minute pressed it to her lips. Her eyes filled with tears.

"What a change!" she murmured. There was deep pathos in her tones.

The photograph was one that she had guarded sacredly. It was a perfect likeness of Phil at the time when he and Marion were passing the happiest days of their lives. She was with him when the picture was taken. It was her presence that gave it the expression she prized so much—the expression that was photographed on her heart never to be effaced.

She stood for a long time under the gas jet, studying the two faces—the one, the photograph in her hand, the other the mental impress of Derringforth as she had seen him tonight.

"How unlike," she said to herself softly, "and only four years. I cannot realize it. The old light, careless nature has gone. How strong and serious his face has grown. It isn't like the old Phil. It doesn't seem possible that such a change could come to any one in so short a time."

If she had known one half of what he had suffered; one half of what he had endured; one half the energy, the dash, the will force he had put forth in combat with bull and bear, she would have seen sufficient cause for the changes in him. One cannot do a man's work without developing the characteristics of a man. Derringforth's experience had been of the kind that brings out the stronger elements of a man's nature. In Wall Street one readily shows the qualities that are in him. There he has the opportunity to display generalship, or bravery, or cowardice. His measure is soon taken; the force of his stroke is quickly learned.

Marion set the picture on the table and sat down before it. As her eyes rested upon it the past came back to her with wonderful vividness. The happy days that she and Phil had enjoyed together from childhood on passed before her in quick review. She saw, even as she had never realized before, the depth of Phil's love for her; the depth of her own love for him. It was unmistakable. Ten thousand examples furnished incontrovertible proof—examples of sacrifice, of consideration, of kindness, of tenderness, and patience, and devotion.

"Oh, why was this ever disturbed?" she cried. "It was cruel, wicked, to break in upon such happiness, to break up such happiness. Mama was blind; I was blind, or I never should have yielded to her wishes. I have had a good deal of pleasure, I know. I don't want to blame mama. She did the best she knew, but she was wrong—oh, how wrong! All the pleasure I have ever had has been but a poor return for that better pleasure—that truer happiness I should have enjoyed with Phil.

"And this is not all. It is only my side. What of Phil? How has it been with him, poor fellow? I could read in his face tonight something of the disappointment he has felt; something of the heartache he must have borne. He has suffered more than I, I am sure. His life has been so different, so sad, losing his father and mother, and then the failure!

"How brave he has been, and how strong and manly he has grown! Yes, it has been a thousand times harder for him than it has been for me! I have been flattered and courted and entertained, but with all this I have not been really happy. I have not escaped without the same pangs of disappointment that Phil has felt. I know what it is to be lonely and restless and dissatisfied—know what it is to love and feel that the man I love has forgotten me forever. The very attention I have had has palled on me and only added to the weariness of my soul. I could not write to Phil; I could do nothing but wait and starve. My whole life, since mama refused to allow me to become engaged, has been false to my very nature. At times —many times—I have felt the intoxication of social triumphs, but never for one minute have I been as happy as in the old days with Phil. I wish I could go back to them again, and forget that I ever knew another life. I wish I could."

Marion repeated the words with a pathetic yearning—a longing that in itself was hopelessness. As her mind flew over the past her emotion became deeper and deeper. She was upon the verge of breaking down. The wintry wind dashed madly against the windows. Marion shuddered half unconsciously at the sound, and murmured:

"Oh, how I wish I could, but it is too late—I know it is too late. He loves her—*Phil loves her.* She is very sweet. He could not help loving her, and she loves him. She is so young and so proud of him; I could see it. Oh, it is so cruel, so cruel!" she cried, giving way at last.

Her head bent forward upon the table, close to the photograph of him she loved, and there, in the silence of the night, and with that heartache to which none other can compare, she sobbed the bitter sobs of despair.

At this same hour, when ghosts are wont to stalk stealthily through the chambers of the living, another girl, younger than Marion and almost as fair, was walking the floor, in the agony of her soul. It was Dorothy. She had seen enough tonight to awaken all the passion of her nature; all the jealousy of love.

The emotion shown alike by Derringforth and Marion, when they met and took each other's hand, kindled into flame all the fire of Dorothy's Southern blood. She saw the expression of their faces—saw that each was moved to such a degree that speech for the moment was impossible. She knew by unerring intuition what this meant.

"Oh, why did I ever meet him?" she cried in bitter anguish. "He loves her, and he has won my heart, my very life. It is so cruel!" she sobbed, "so cruel! He might have told me—might have warned me against this fate—this worse than death. She is so beautiful, so attractive! He never could care for me as he does for her—never could love me so long as she lives. But I thought he did love me. Could I have been so blind? Did he deceive himself and think for a time that he did love me? If not—if his words, his looks, his devotion—if the pressure of his lips upon my hand was not love, then oh, how blind I was! I cannot believe him so heartless—so wicked. He has always seemed so sincere, so noble. I have trusted him and loved him with all my heart. He must be true. I won't believe him so vile. It cannot be; it shall not be."

Hope began to revive. The gloom was less dense. She recalled everything that would tend to show he loved her. The evidence multiplied, and the case brightened. The color again gave life to her face, and with throbbing heart she felt once more confident of Derringforth's loyalty and love.

Then suddenly the picture of his meeting with Marion flashed before her eyes, and again she found herself groping in darkness. This time she went even to a lower depth of hopelessness than before, and saw in Derringforth the exemplification of depravity so black, so cunning, so horrible, that she hid her face in her hands in very fear.

She got up and began walking the floor. Her nerves were at highest tension. Presently she stopped before the mirror, and after a moment murmured, "He can never care for me. Her eyes would win any man, and then she is so tall and graceful. Look at my baby face, and then see the character in hers. If only I were as clever, I wouldn't mind so much; then perhaps it would be different. She has every advantage. There is no hope for me. I can't blame him, though I ought to, for he has ruined my life. There will never be any more happiness for me, but she will be so happy!"

LI.

DERRINGFORTH had barely reached Dorothy when the house was thrown into confusion. A fire had broken out from some combustible material in the cellar, and smoke was beginning to pour into the ball room from the furnace flues. In another minute all was excitement. The dance was broken up, and the women made a stampede for their dressing room, while the men turned to fight the growing flames.

Derringforth was foremost among the number, and went at the work with that same dash that had always characterized his movements. The fight was of short duration. The fire was soon under control, but not soon enough to save Derringforth from a drenching. He was wet to the skin with the icy water of winter. When he came up from the scene of the diminutive conflagration, Marion and Dorothy, with most of the other guests, had gone. He had to wait a few minutes for his carriage. The wind swept through the awning and stiffened his wet clothes into ice. His rooms were cold when he reached them, and for the first time in his life he learned the sensation of a genuine chill.

In a little while he was in a burning fever. He tossed restlessly on his pillow, and with a frightful headache thought with an intensity that was almost consuming. One look at Dorothy when he returned to her from Marion was enough to convince him of her love. He needed no further evidence. The pained expression of her sweet young face appealed to him with exceptional force. He felt an impulse to take her in his arms and assure her of his love. But the place did not permit of such demonstration; neither did their relations warrant it. For the moment Marion was forgotten. Dorothy had touched his sympathy, even as Marion had touched it a little while before. Then came the alarm of fire, the confusion, and the effort to extinguish the flames.

Now he was alone; and freed from the personal influence of either the one or the other he began to reason logically—began to realize the delicacy of his position. That both Dorothy and Marion loved him there could be no doubt. That he loved both was equally certain. He could not shut his eyes to this fact. For the one his love was fresher; for the other deeper.

Was he glad that Dorothy loved him? Yes and no. Had he not met Marion again, there would have been but one answer. Dorothy had come into his life when he was starving. His soul was filled with cynicism and gloom. One touch of her hand,

and these vanished, and life was bright again. No man of human instincts could have helped loving her. She was as sweet and refreshing as the sunshine. Youth and refinement and beauty such as hers would have conquered a stoic.

Derringforth was intensely human. He would not have been good for anything were he not. He was a man. Dorothy admired him, and love went out from heart to heart. She gave him all without reserve. He gave her all that was his to give. He could do no more. Time could never efface the impress of Marion. It had grown with his growth, and was a part of life itself—not the fickle Marion of his fancy, but the real Marion as he had known her—as she was in fact.

Ten thousand loves combined could never equal this one — this first one that God willed and guided. Life is not long enough by a million years to blot out such a love. There are not many of them — not many that begin with life itself and develop to such perfection as this one between Marion and Phil had reached when misguided ambition stepped in to thwart the will of Heaven.

One look into Marion's eyes, the pressure of her hand within his own, and all the miserable caricatures of her—the creations of disordered fancy—were swept away, and he blushed with shame for the injustice he had done her. The Marion of his youth, the same sweet, beautiful girl, was before him, and the old love that had been beaten back by his strong will sprang from the deep recesses of his heart and thrilled him with a delight that was worth the living of a life to know.

This, then, was the complication Derringforth had to face. He was not guilty of wrong. He had supposed that Marion had abandoned all thought of him forever. If he had known or suspected the constancy of her love, or even dreamed of it, nothing on earth could have induced him to encourage Dorothy's love.

But that which had been done could not be undone. Regrets were idle. The past, with all its mistakes, was as fixed as the everlasting hills. The future, with its bearings on the past, was the problem he must solve.

While these thoughts were surging through his feverish brain, Marion was bowed before his likeness in deep and somber reverie. At length the cold, gray light of the wintry morning, sifting in through the soft curtain, aroused her. What torture she had suffered! How keen the pangs of a dying hope! With a soul like death, with benumbed limbs and haggard features, she struggled to her feet and started to move away. Then she stopped and turned back to the table, and with trembling hands took up Phil's photograph and pressed it once more to her lips. There was something in the way she did this—something so sad, so utterly sorrowful in her expression, that it was as a last farewell to one whose life was to her more than her own.

She held the picture a little way off and gazed longingly at it. She pressed it still again to her lips, and with a pathetic cry reeled and fell heavily upon the floor.

LII.

WHEN Derringforth returned to Wall Street from his enforced vacation at Colonel Rayburn's Virginia home, he was confronted by a condition of things that few men would care to face. An indebtedness of two million dollars, with assets to the extent of about half this sum, presented the problem before him.

He was twenty four. An older head would have hesitated before entering upon such a task. But old heads do not always mean stanch hearts. Youth dares where mature age yields to caution.

But the indebtedness before Derringforth was not all. A man of force makes strong friends and strong enemies. To have everybody's friendship is to be a dead level sort of man—a man without individuality, without fire. Derringforth had square corners; had directness. He worked on a straight line. He would rather tunnel a mountain than go around it or over it. Any obstacle smaller than a mountain he felt like forcing aside.

These characteristics won the admiration of many

and the hatred of those who had to stand aside or smart for their folly. No man could do what Derringforth had done in Wall Street without running up against a good many of this latter class. He was always courteous ; always affable ; always surcharged with kinetic energy. Had he been less aggressive, less forceful, he might now have been worth an assured fortune. But he preferred bankruptcy to being a trimmer. He knew only one course of action, and that was along the lines of his nature. There was a sincerity and honesty in this that men were compelled to admire—even those who suffered from the force of his stroke.

Derringforth's affairs were in about as bad shape as they could well be in when he stretched forth his hand, for the first time after weeks of idleness, to begin the work of righting them. He found two factions ; the one welcoming him back to the Street with a friendly smile, the other receiving him with so chilly an atmosphere that it would have frozen into inaction the courage of most men.

But not so with Derringforth. There was a mental gritting of the teeth—a tingling of the blood along his veins, that meant mischief to those who sought to crush him.

If he could have undertaken the work of straightening out his affairs immediately after his failure, as he had intended doing, the task would have been comparatively easy. His long absence gave his enemies time to work up an opposition to him that only a strong personality and stanch integrity could overcome.

This is the way he began the work before him. "I am not a very old man," he said to his creditors. "You know something of my record—perhaps everything. I hope everything; if not, I shall be glad to give you any information you may desire. I have made some money, as you know; I have made it reasonably fast. I have come back to make some more; to pay off my obligations—to pay in full every dollar I owe—every penny, interest and all. The time necessary to see this purpose an accomplished fact depends to a considerable extent on you, gentlemen—on the terms of settlement you may conclude among yourselves to be wisest and most just to yourselves. An engine with a few pounds of steam makes slow progress on an up grade, but with steam enough to work it to its full capacity, it knows no grades. All the money I have is practically in your hands. It is beyond mine. I shall suggest that it, or such proportion of it as you consider advisable, be turned over to you without further delay than legal formalities make necessary. The sooner a basis of settlement can be agreed upon, the sooner I can begin the work of meeting my obligations. I hope you will fix upon this basis with the least possible delay. I am anxious to pull off my coat and get to work."

"We like it," was the verdict of Derringforth's

friendly creditors. "There is metal in that young man," they said. "There is force there. He has that sort of manliness that wins; that sort of confidence in himself that wins."

But the opposing element, those who had felt the force of Derringforth's will, and those closest to Van Stump, attempted to make it appear that Derringforth's words were mere braggadocio—the drivel of irresponsibility, the utterance of disgusting conceit.

Van Stump had put himself in such relations with certain of Derringforth's creditors that he could seriously block the way to a rational settlement. It had cost him a fortune to break Derringforth, and now that the young financier was down he proposed to keep him down, if the force of his influence, and any reasonable expenditure of money, would do it.

Derringforth had not been in New York many days when he had gathered a very clear idea of the situation. He was able to trace the opposition to its source, and found a sense of grim delight in Van Stump's personal antagonism.

"It will give me all the more satisfaction to get back at him when I strike my pace once more," he said to himself with a smile. It was one of those smiles that few men would care to have to face. There was a certain squareness of the jaw suggestive of that sort of determination which it is well not to run up against.

This was Van Stump's inning. He enjoyed it.

The fight between the two factions—the friends and the enemies of Derringforth—went merrily on, and the days slipped by with no apparent progress toward a settlement.

At length Colonel Rayburn and others of Derringforth's friends became incensed at the nasty spirit of the obstructionists, and determined to make short work of their game. The antagonistic faction represented a total of about four hundred thousand dollars of Derringforth's two millions of indebtedness. A meeting of the creditors was called, and every claim was represented. The opposition was there in force, and came prepared to obstruct any movement that looked toward a rational settlement.

Derringforth was there. He had been requested to be there. One of his friends arose and urged the desirability of treating him with the consideration that honesty and energy deserve. This brought forth a determined protest from the Van Stump faction.

Presently Colonel Rayburn got up, and with flashing eyes and scathing irony held these enemies of Derringforth's up to the view of all present. He was not especially considerate of their feelings in the choice of his words, which were such as best expressed his contempt for those who would lend themselves to a despicable persecution. Then, turning to Derringforth, he said:

"It is my pleasure, Mr. Derringforth, on behalf of several gentlemen present, and also on my own behalf, to hand you herewith a complete release from all your indebtedness to us. These papers will show you the parties to this release, who represent about sixteen hundred thousand dollars of your indebtedness. This will enable you to pay off in full the remaining four hundred thousand, and leave you a balance of six hundred thousand dollars as a capital on which to resume business. This step on the part of my associates and myself is taken with pleasure, and you have our best wishes and our thorough confidence for your future."

"This action on your part, Colonel Rayburn, and on the part of those who have acted with you," said Derringforth, taking the papers from Colonel Rayburn's hand, "has come to me with a suddenness that almost robs me of speech. It has been my good fortune to know something of your kindness before, and I have known of like kindness on the part of some of the gentlemen associated with you in this action, but I could never have expected anything so incomparably generous at your hands. You have surprised and overwhelmed me. I cannot realize in so brief a time the full extent of your kindness. I can only thank you, and assure you that the magnanimity of your act in canceling my obligations so far as legal claim bears upon me, has placed me under others which can never be repaid. The money I owe you I shall return, both principal and interest, and I shall do this, I believe, in so short a time that you will feel you have discovered a wiser principle in dealing with the man who is down than the one that generally obtains. But that other obligation—the one that gives me a new and better conception of my fellow man—can never be canceled. I am proud to be under such obligation; I am proud to have your confidence, gentlemen. I shall not abuse it. Again I thank you."

A cheer that would have thrilled the soul of a cynic burst forth from the lips of Colonel Rayburn and his associates, and each in turn pressed forward and grasped Derringforth's hand and with warmest congratulations wished him a world of prosperity. While this was going on, the obstructionists, with the exception of half a dozen, slunk from the room. Of those who remained, one rapped for attention and said:

"I think I am a wiser man than when I came into this meeting; I hope I am a better one. If kindlier impulses indicate an improvement, then I am better. I have been hit hard; I deserved it. What I have seen done here today has impressed me as nothing in a decade has done before. I want to be one of you, gentlemen. I want to subscribe my name with yours to that release."

Again the room rang with applause, and still again there was cause for rejoicing, for the other five obstructionists came forward and asked that they too might join with Derringforth's friends.

It was one of those rare occasions when good feeling rises to sublime heights, and nobler impulses thrill the soul with inspiration almost divine. Every one of those now present went out from that meeting a bigger man, with bigger conceptions and a sunnier slant; those who had slunk away were meaner and more groveling than before.

The additional half dozen releases reduced Derringforth's legal obligations to somewhat less than two hundred thousand dollars. With eight hundred thousand as a working capital, and a credit made almost limitless by the faith shown in him by his creditors, he was magnificently equipped for the great Wall Street arena.

He entered it with a stride that bespoke confidence, and his hand was felt in more than one important deal before nightfall. One week had scarcely passed before he had rolled up a profit of fifty thousand dollars; one week had not passed when the creditors who had treated him so generously began to reap the fruits of their broad policy—they had Derringforth's check for a payment of ten per cent of that which he owed them.

When Van Stump learned of the break in the forces arrayed against Derringforth, and of the action of his leading creditors, the fire flew from his little, steel gray eyes. He walked back and forth in his room, in a rage. Martin Strum, the smooth man of long suffering qualities, had just entered the august presence of his master, and was setting forth well laid plans for squeezing the life blood from another business house as it had once been squeezed from the Derringforths.

"These are clients worth your consideration," he had just said, with an artificial smile. "I have never brought you such clients before, and it was by the merest chance that I discovered their needs—needs, yes, that's it. They are in just that condition where they will yield to any demands so long as they get the relief they seek."

There was unusual spirit in Strum's manner this morning. He was less obsequious than usual—less humble. The sight of this fine old business house, with pride in its history of a century and more to uphold—the sight of the Van Stump grasp tightening around this aristocratic throat—was enough to quicken the cold, sluggish blood in his miserable veins. Scarcely fifteen minutes after entering into the sacred presence of his principal, he slid out feeling as if he had suddenly run up against that portion of a mule in which marvelous energy is centered. Metaphorically considered, there were stars shooting wildly throughout the firmament, and he was not quite sure whether he was Martin Strum or the fragment of a comet whirling madly through space. There was a dizziness about his brain that paralyzed his senses.

LIII.

THERE is a point at which nature rebels and breaks. Marion had reached that point. An eternity of torture had been compressed into a few hours. The agony of a broken heart was stilled for a time.

It was toward night. The sun had traversed the heavens and was sinking in the west. On one side of the bed on which Marion lay was the old family physician. There was deep anxiety in his face as he watched her—an anxiety that filled the hearts of Mr. and Mrs. Kingsley with despair. They were close to Marion's side, and were watching eagerly every movement of her lips, as she uttered the rambling words that pierced her mother's heart.

"'How will it be at the end of a year?' Oh, Phil, Phil! how can you speak such cruel words? Does mama object to you? Mama thinks the world of you. You should know that as you know I love you, so how can a year's delay change us? I know your love is too true to be shaken in that time. If it were not—oh, Phil, I cannot bear to think of it! Such thoughts break my heart. Can't you see, don't you know that nothing in the world would make me so happy as to be your wife? This love is not new to you and me, Phil. We have been lovers all our lives, and I have always looked forward to the time when my school days would end, thinking you and I would then be more to each other than ever.

"And now they are over, we are less to each other, you say. No, Phil, that is not so. We are not less to each other. We never shall be less to each other. It is hard enough to yield to mama without your making it harder.

"You don't wish to make it harder, you say. I know you don't. I am so sorry for you, Phil, dear, so sorry for myself, but what can I do? You would not have me marry against mama's wishes, I am sure, and yet you think it might be best. Phil, you shock me. I must not allow you to say such things—it is wicked, horrible. Just think what you have said. And then you say we cannot look into the future; we cannot tell what changes a year will make in us, in our nature, in our surroundings, in our tastes. I know we cannot tell exactly, Phil, but I know that you and I will not cease to love each other whatever else happens, and mama will give her consent for us to marry. It is only a year, Phil. The time will go very quickly. You can spend every evening with me, and I will go down town and come home with you now and then at night, and I will try to make you just the happiest boy in the world. Now, you will be good and wait patiently, won't you ; wait for my sake, and for mama's sake? She thinks the world of you, Phil, and she will not ask us to wait after the year is over. I am sure she won't."

These were bitter words for Mrs. Kingsley's ears. She shuddered as they fell from Marion's lips. Each sentence was condemnation. The fruits of her folly had come home to her in a way she little expected. It required all the strength she could summon to remain and listen to this terrible revelation. Marion continued, in pleading, plaintive tones.

"I should think you might come with us, Phil—with me—you say you wish you could," she went on, now resentfully, " but that it is impossible. Impossible ! " she repeated, with weird force and frowning brow. "Love should know no impossibilities. Do I question your love, you ask? No, Phil, no, I do not question it, but ought you to refuse me anything ? Would I refuse you anything ? Yes, I did refuse you something once, I know," she admitted, with changed expression, " but it was not my fault. I had to obey mama. You agreed with me that there was no other way and promised to help me to wait patiently. Let us not go on in this way, Phil. Let us avoid these things that might cause us regret," and she reached out her hand as if extending it to him in token of good faith.

The tears rolled down Mrs. Kingsley's face, and Mr. Kingsley could scarcely bear up under the strain. It was something to shake the nerves even of the old physician, who had witnessed many pathetic scenes in his long professional career.

"I ought to tell Phil all about Burton Edwards, I know," continued Marion, "but I cannot quite make up my mind to do it. He should have my confidence, of course. I have been a little wicked, perhaps, but I didn't mean any harm. I really didn't want Burton to become interested in me. I wish I could tell Phil. Love should have no secrets. I am sure he would not blame me, and yet it is so hard, I cannot seem to begin the confession. Phil doesn't seem the same. He is so distant, so far away from me. I wonder if I have been drifting away from him. If we keep on in this way—but I won't think of it. I will not allow anything to separate Phil from me." Then, as if holding a letter before her eyes, she read: "'I hope you can give me next Thursday evening. The year we were asked to wait will have passed. I know you are very busy socially, but the matter for us to consider means much to you and me, Marion.'

"I wish Phil had not added this last sentence. It hurts me. I know he doesn't mean to hurt me, but he does. I wonder if I have changed as much as he has, and mama is not willing that I should become engaged to Phil even now. I told him a year ago that we should have to wait only one year, and that mama would give her consent then. Yes, only one year. How long it seemed, and now it has gone.

Did I tell Phil the truth? I intended to be truthful and thought I was, but mama makes no secret with me now of her dislike for Phil, and she is more bitterly opposed to my engagement than ever. What shall I say to Phil? Oh, dear me, I wish I had been engaged a year ago. I wish I had not yielded to mama's wishes, but I could not do anything else, and now, must I disobey her or must I break Phil's heart? It is so much worse than it was then."

Mrs. Kingsley turned away from the bed in bitter agony, and, leaning on the arm of her husband, sank crushed upon the couch.

"You must not remain here," said the physician. "I cannot permit it. The strain will kill you."

"No, no," said Mrs. Kingsley, waving him away; "I cannot go. It is my place to be here. *The potion is mine. I must drink it.*"

"Come with me, dear," said Mr. Kingsley tenderly. "Your presence will not help Marion, and her wanderings are more than you can bear."

But Mrs. Kingsley was deaf to these appeals, and leaned forward that she might catch every word from Marion's lips.

"Oh, that look!" exclaimed Marion, putting up her hands as if to hide the face from her eyes. "How it condemns me!" and a shudder shook her fevered frame. The tears stole down her cheeks, and between sobs she moaned, "I know I have been doing wrong in breathing this atmosphere of love. I did not do it wilfully. I had the impulse to fly from Burton, and yet there was something that seemed to tie me to him. How Phil's look pierces me. Poor fellow! I pity him! I have been very wicked, and yet I have not been wilfully wrong. It seems as if something were constantly leading me away from Phil against my will. Oh, it was such a mistake postponing the engagement! We were so happy then, and would have been so happy! All this torture, this frightful heartache would have been avoided."

Presently she continued as if talking to herself: " How cold and distant he is! He is keeping something from me," and a look of jealousy came into her expression. Then she went on: " I did not think business would keep you from coming to see me. Would it have kept you a year ago, I wonder?" There was censure in her tones. She shuddered as if from the very coldness of his manner.

" If mama was right a year ago, you say, why should not she wish the same policy to prevail for another year, and perhaps yet another, and maybe still another?

" Mama thinks she was right.

" Yes, I have talked with her about it. I am so sorry, but what can I do? You would not wish me to disobey her, I am sure.

" Yes, I know I said the same thing a year ago, but I said it in good faith. I believed mama meant that we should become engaged now, or I should not have told you so. I have never deceived you, Phil—not exactly. There are some things I have wanted to tell you, but you have been so distant I could not seem to approach you. The very words froze in my mouth. I do not think I am altogether to blame. Won't you blame yourself just a little, and make it easier for me? Tell me that you have drifted away from me, so that I won't think that I have done all the drifting. Papa is willing we should become engaged. He was willing a year ago, but it was mama who stood between us. I know she did what seemed best for us, but she was wrong—oh, how wrong she was! You do not know, Phil, how I have suffered. You never can know. I have thought sometimes that I would tell you, but, as I just said, the words refused to come. And then you never came to see me before I went to Europe. It was like tearing out my heart to go away without seeing you, Phil. Why didn't you come to me? I would have left the steamer even, if you had come to me and shown me that you loved me. I should have been so happy. But no, you didn't come—you didn't answer my letter—didn't care, it seemed to me, where I went. Was I happy—happy, you say? How could I be happy without you? I tried to seem happy—tried to make mama think I was happy, but it wasn't like the old happiness we used to enjoy, Phil. Oh, for just one more summer like the old summers when you and I were together in the country. But it is too late—too late. There will never be any more such pleasure for me. *She* will have you with her and she will be so happy. It is almost more than I can bear, Phil. It doesn't seem right. I don't blame you, and yet it is so cruel—so unjust—unjust "——

Marion's words had been growing more and more indistinct and were now scarcely audible. The opiate administered by the doctor had begun its quieting effect. Her eyes, that had flashed their wavering, unrecognizing glances on those standing by her side, fluttered feebly and then closed. She lay there, pallid, still, almost as one dead.

Mrs. Kingsley's face was white and haggard. She had seen herself as the destroyer of her own daughter's happiness, if not her very life. With fear and anxiety and bitter self condemnation she struggled to her feet, and bending over the bed looked down upon Marion. She stood there motionless, with all the agony of supreme suffering in her face. Presently her lips moved and framed the soundless words: "My own folly! My own folly! Oh, God, have pity on her, my child."

LIV.

WHILE Marion was wandering in mind, Derringforth was struggling in body against a formidable attack of pneumonia. Colonel Rayburn noted his absence from the Street, and, knowing of his exposure on the previous night, at once became anxious. He lost little time in going personally to Derringforth's rooms, where he found the latter in the hands of a trained nurse.

A .week later, when Derringforth had recovered sufficiently to be moved with safety, he was taken to Colonel Rayburn's home on Riverside Drive. He had rebelled against this, but the kindness and solicitude of Colonel and Mrs. Rayburn, and the messages of cheer from Dorothy, were impelling forces not to be resisted. He yielded, and fate again smiled at the cunning of its handiwork.

His own mother could not have done more for him than Mrs. Rayburn ; his own sister, had God blessed him with one, could not have ministered more tenderly to his comfort than did Dorothy. Her presence was sunshine ; her words more potent than the potions of the physician. As returning health began coursing through his veins, Derringforth realized that he had been drifting from Marion toward Dorothy. It seemed to him that this drifting had taken him out of the natural channel of his life, and yet his environment, and his obligations to Dorothy, checked the impulse to protest. It was not as if he did not love Dorothy. Without this love he would have found some good reason for gently discouraging her love. As it was, he had not the heart to do this, and each day he saw, sometimes with a feeling of regret, sometimes with a thrill of joy, that her life was more and more firmly welded to his.

Her childlike confidence in him appealed to his sense of honor, while, at the same time, her bright face and gentle manner quickened his admiration for this sweet flower of the sunny South. There was but one outcome to the inexorable logic of the situation, and yet there was an undercurrent in the very fiber of Derringforth's nature that rebelled against this outcome. At times he almost dreaded the approach of Dorothy, whose step, but for one haunting fancy, was music to his ear.

He could not banish Marion from his mind. Much of his thought, during the hours of convalescence, was of her. The old days of happiness were lived over and over, with a realism that made him dead to the present. She was his ideal, his other half—the God created other half, and yet he could not take unto himself his own. If he could only discover defects in Dorothy's character that would modify his feeling for her, then he might see his way to a pretext for casting off the cords that were drawing him to a destiny not his own.

"Oh, why was I permitted to meet Marion again?" he cried out in bitter anguish. And yet he was conscious of a longing to see her—a longing that was consuming his very soul.

The days went by and he heard nothing from her. At first he wondered at this, and then he began to speculate as to the cause of her silence. And out of this reasoning rose the image of Devonshire.

A cloud darkened Derringforth's brow. He recalled his own bitter feelings when Devonshire broke in upon Marion and himself just at that time when each was beginning to see through the mist and into the true nature of the other. He remembered the gracious welcome Marion gave the tall Englishman, and a throb of jealousy racked his enfeebled frame. From this point he began to view Marion through the cynical eyes that cruelly belied her.

He had been very ill and his friends—his true friends, had come to him, while Marion, so far as he knew, had not given him a thought. He fancied her under the spell of the Englishman, and wondered that she could at one moment be the old sweet Marion and at another be so untrue to herself.

This view of Marion had crept stealthily into Derringforth's mind. He had tried to force it back, but it reasserted itself always, and with darker shadings. The contrast between this perverted fancy of Marion, and Dorothy's sweet young face, beaming with sincerity and love, was potent in bending Derringforth's steps toward the path fate had blazed for him.

LV.

A FEW hours after Burton Edwards left Marion in the ball room, and before the day had fully dawned, a monster engine dashed into the black mouth of the tunnel at Sixty Seventh Street, and with a savage snort dragged a train load of human souls in after it. In the rear coach a young man sat, bowed and bent, and half buried in a mammoth coat with huge collar that completely covered the back of his head. A cap was drawn well down over his forehead, almost hiding the eyes. His hands were lost in a pair of great, deep breast pockets. One foot was thrown up indifferently on the seat in front of him, and the other rested listlessly upon the floor of the car. This young man was Burton Edwards—dejected, dispirited, broken hearted.

Had he taken any other train than this particular one he might have been back in the metropolis again at the end of the day, and once more hovering about Marion with that same passionate love that burned as a mighty volcano within him. The fact that he had left her at a moment when he had suddenly become disheartened, did not signify that he might not as suddenly discover that he had acted rashly. Indeed he had scarcely passed beyond the Harlem when this suspicion began to take shape within his brain, and as he skirted the Hudson, flying at a mad speed toward Albany, the feeling developed into one of actual regret. Something whispered into his ear: "It is not yet too late," and his face brightened. "But my trunks," he exclaimed, and his brow became perplexed.

The porter just then passed by. Edwards called to him, and handing him half a dollar sent him hurriedly to the baggage car in search of information.

"They may have gone on the first section," Edwards reflected dubiously. "I couldn't go back to New York without them. It would be awkward enough, any way. I wish I hadn't written those notes. My friends will imagine me on my way to San Francisco. Well, so I am—ticketed through. I wish I hadn't been such an idiot. Why hasn't Derringforth married Marion, if he loves her so much? Perhaps he loves the other girl. A fellow ought not to say die, any way. I was a blamed ass. I'm not afraid of the Englishman, but why in thunder he always turns up in my way is a mystery. He haunts me."

The porter pushed through the doorway, and swung along the aisle. Edwards looked up eagerly into the black face.

"Gone on the first section, sir, and I s'pect you kayn't stop 'em now, leastwise not before Syracuse."

Edwards' countenance fell. He raved a little mentally. What should he do? Between swearing at himself and cursing Devonshire, he kept on asking himself this question until Albany was reached. By this time he was well befogged with irresolution. He was upon the point of leaving the car, thinking he would telegraph to Syracuse to have his trunks detained.

He stood up and looked out of the window. He reached for his umbrella. There was nothing but indecision in that reach. Just then a young woman came into the car, accompanied by her father and mother. Edwards saw her and hesitated. As she walked up the aisle toward him her eyes met his. Somehow or other the umbrella was back in its place in another instant, and with a flush of confusion he sat down, wondering if she had noticed his sudden change of mind, and realized the cause.

The engine gave a shrill, sharp whistle and sent up a few mighty puffs. The wheels began to turn and the train shot forward toward the great West, bearing Edwards every minute farther and farther away from the metropolis and Marion. But perhaps this thought did not occur to him just at this time. The young woman, whose beauty had swerved him from his vacillation, was settling herself, as if for a long journey, in the section directly opposite his.

"The gods are with me for once," he said to himself, scarcely able to restrain a smile. The sluggish beat of his heart was quickened, and there came into his face a look of delight that was seen from the corners of a pair of mischievous eyes across the aisle.

"I wonder who she is?" thought Edwards.

"I wonder who he is?" thought the young woman.

"By Jove, she is sweet!" exclaimed Edwards in a burst of enthusiasm.

"Isn't he handsome!" she said, her admiration already astir.

"This is luck! I'm playing to a great house," reflected Edwards.

"How strange that he should be directly opposite me!" continued his vis-à-vis, "and what a picturesque fellow he is."

"She dresses mighty well and has a figure worth dressing—willowy. I verily believe I could span her waist with my hands—Jove, what coloring and what eyes!"

"I wonder if he is going West too—looks just like a Western boy—jolly, I'm sure."

"If only she were bound for California! But no, that would be a royal flush, and a fellow hardly strikes one in a lifetime."

"Perhaps this may not be such a stupid journey after all."

"I wonder if I shall meet her! Devilish exasperating to be so close to a girl and be debarred by conventionality from speaking to her. Civilization has its weak spots."

"But then we might travel side by side, I suppose, for three thousand miles," continued mademoiselle, "and get no nearer to each other. How absurd it is!"

"There must be some way for me to bring this about without making a break," went on Edwards. "I wonder how other men have made acquaintances on trains? I've read about them, but conditions differ so."

"I wish I knew where he is from. He may be a friend of friends of mine."

"Who is there in Albany that I know? Blamed if I can remember ever having known any one from there! I don't see how I can work this scheme, then."

"He was on the train when we came in and must be from New York. I wonder if he knows Dorothy? Wouldn't it be odd, and here we are, side by side—and as glum as mummies."

"But it won't do to hurry the thing. It will be all up with me if I do," and with this reflection Edwards reached down, and opening his valise took out a novel and made a show of reading it.

Mademoiselle chatted lightly with her mother and was evidently in the best of spirits. Time went by, and Edwards had perfunctorily scanned a hundred pages of his novel. Presently he heard the mother exclaim:

"Oh, Eleanor, see that horse cut up! He is frightened—there, he has overturned the carriage!"

"So her name is Eleanor," mused Edwards, with a smile of satisfaction. "Well, this is a beginning."

But beyond this, advancement was discouragingly slow, and he found himself wondering why he had allowed this girl to influence him in the slightest degree.

"She is the most indifferent being I ever saw. She has hardly looked this way since she came into the car. Might as well think of making the acquaintance of a sphinx. Here I am almost at Buffalo, and my trunks will have gone on when I reach there. There is nothing to do but go on myself, I suppose. Not so much of a cinch as I thought. Girls give a man no end of trouble. I've chased over two continents for Marion, and upon my soul I don't believe she would marry me if she knew by so doing she would save my life. And yet, somehow or other, it is hard for me to really believe this. If I had I shouldn't have been idiot enough to do as I have done. I wish I had gone back to New York. I should have done so, I suppose, but for this girl. I thought she was human. These people in the East are icy. They fairly freeze all one's best impulses."

Eleanor's father was a quiet, studious man. He had taken a seat at the further end of the car and was lost to his surroundings in a book. Edwards had hoped to see him go to the smoking room, thinking to join him there, where the comradeship of the cigar places fellow travelers on easy terms.

"But he is too cold to indulge in this bit of luxury," growled Edwards. "He must have come from New England, where the sun shines grudgingly."

The night closed in about them, and with the lighting up of the car there came a vague sense of the drawing room. The world was shut out by the curtained windows, and a suggestion of the family circle stole over Edwards. He felt himself drawn nearer to the strangers across the aisle. But the hours slipped by, and at length the berths were made up for the night. Weary of the effort to meet Eleanor, he went into the smoking room, where he fell back on the companionship of the cigar in place of that better companionship he had thus far failed to win.

When he returned to his section, Eleanor had gone to bed; so had her father and mother.

"It's all up with me," he reflected. "We shall probably take different routes at Chicago, and I shall never see her again. I wish I had not seen her at all. She is a beautiful girl. I cannot forget her face."

Edwards had had no sleep the night before, and it was late the next morning when he awoke. He was still in the dressing room when the train ran into the station in Chicago. He hurried back to his section, only to find Eleanor with her father and mother leaving the car. As she passed through the doorway she turned her head slightly and looked back. Finding his eyes following her, her face flushed, and the suggestion of a smile that was half regret, half mischief, added a piquancy to her beauty that set Edwards' heart throbbing madly.

He quickly gathered up his effects and hurried out, hoping that he might again see her, but when he reached the platform she had disappeared.

There was no time to be lost if he wished to catch the connecting train for the West. In another minute he was whirling across the city in a cab, and cursing his luck that he did not wake up earlier. After reaching the station he found he had a few minutes before the train started, and he lighted a cigar and walked up and down the platform, his brow knit. He wondered if by any chance he would ever see Eleanor again—where she was from, where she was going, and what her last name was.

"With sixty five millions of people in this country there is very little likelihood of my ever running across her. If I had only learned her full name I would have a show. Why didn't I have brains enough to ask the porter? I always think of things just when it is too late."

From Eleanor his mind drifted back to Marion and the ball room, where he left her with Derringforth.

"It is folly for me to think of her in any other sense than as a friend," he reflected. "I believe she cares a good deal for me in this way, but not in the way she cares for Derringforth. It is best for me to keep on home. I should have returned to New York, I fancy, but for Eleanor. Though I never see her again, I should thank her within my heart for this influence, slight as it was, that held me to my original purpose."

His long devotion to Marion—the persistency with which he had clung to the hope that he might yet win her love, was inconsistent with his very nature. It was accident rather than character. The staying quality that marks the steady stroke was not his. He had the enthusiasm of a girl, and a temperament scarcely less impressionable. But his ranch life had not afforded him the opportunity of social intercourse. He had seen little of girls until he met Marion.

Then, on his visits to the East, he was always in touch with her. In her presence, breathing the atmosphere of her delightful personality, he was blind to the charms of others. Absent from her, he was absent from society.

"All aboard," called the conductor, and the train began to move.

Edwards threw away his cigar and entered the coach, still thinking how odd it was that a stranger —a girl whose face he had never seen before—should play any part in deciding him on a course that would perhaps affect his whole future. He had walked a third of the way down the aisle, paying no heed to any one, when suddenly his eyes met Eleanor's. There she was with her father and mother, and on his very car. His face flushed; so did hers, and he went on to his section, just beyond, with the feeling that the barriers of the day before were giving way.

When people have traveled together for a certain length of time the stiffness in the atmosphere that permeates the car at first insensibly softens, and strangers readily become companions. Almost before Edwards realized it he found himself in conversation with Eleanor's father, and then in a little while with Eleanor herself and her mother.

The Donaldsons—for this was their name—were on their way to California on a pleasure trip. They were Bostonians. Mr. Donaldson had retired from business, and was seeking in travel recreation from the strain of an active career.

Edwards found them most congenial company, and they, on their part, were delighted to fall in with a Californian. But aside from this, Edwards' engaging personality and abounding spirits made him a capital traveling companion. He became one of the quartet in the dining car, and, in fact, he and the Donaldsons were inseparable throughout the rest of the journey.

Eleanor proved quite as charming a girl as the first impress of her face had foreshadowed. She and Edwards were not long in finding many themes of mutual interest. Gradually their conversation drifted to New

York, and Eleanor asked him if he knew Dorothy Rayburn.

Edwards answered in the negative, and then Eleanor sang Dorothy's praises until he began to think he had missed meeting the most delightful girl in New York.

On arriving in California, the Donaldsons went direct to Santa Barbara, while Edwards hurried on home. A week later he was with Eleanor, and after a delightful visit of ten days he persuaded the Donaldsons to become his guests at his father's ranch. There quickly sprang up between the two families a warm friendship, and the same sentiment that pervaded the scenes enacted three years before by Burton Edwards and Marion Kingsley breathed through like scenes reënacted by Burton Edwards and Eleanor Donaldson.

LVI.

THE soft sunshine of the approaching spring came in through the curtained window and played in flickering shadows upon the pale, thin face of Marion Kingsley. She was sitting in a large easy chair, propped up with pillows. Her well rounded figure was emaciated from the long illness that had brought her almost to the verge of the grave.

Near her sat her mother, now older by a dozen years than on that winter day, scarcely three months before, when she heard the words from Marion's unconscious lips that arraigned her as the destroyer of her daughter's happiness.

The postman's whistle had just sounded. Marion gave little heed to the shrill notes. It had been a long time since she had received a letter that had aroused any interest in her. Presently the maid appeared and handed two envelopes to Marion. She took them indifferently, and with a listless air her eyes fell upon the superscription of the topmost one. They rested there only long enough to notice that the writing was unfamiliar to her. She dropped it into her lap in a way that seemed to say, "It is hardly worth the opening."

Then her eyes scanned the address on the other letter. Instantly her white cheeks brightened. A quick flash of hope came into her eyes, and with nervous fingers she tore open the envelope.

The letter was from Derringforth. It ran as follows:

DEAR MARION:
You are my oldest friend, our friendship dating back almost to the beginning of life. For this reason I wish you to be the first among my friends to learn of my engagement. The sweet girl who has promised to be my wife is Dorothy Rayburn, the daughter of Colonel Rayburn. I doubt if you know her, but I hope that you and she may meet very soon and that a firm, deep friendship may grow up between you two. Nothing could now add more to my happiness than this, and I am sure that when Miss Rayburn knows you as I do she will join me in this hope.
Very sincerely yours,
PHIL DERRINGFORTH.
Thursday, the eighth.

The color that had come into Marion's face fled before she had read half a dozen lines, and her pallor was as the pallor of death. Her head fell back upon the pillow, and she lay there helpless, hopeless, with a heart that was dead within her breast.

"My dear, what has happened?" cried Mrs.

Kingsley, trembling violently as she hurried to Marion's aid.

The latter made no reply. There was a stony look of agony in her eyes as she stared into vacancy, but by way of response she pointed a trembling hand toward Derringforth's letter, which had dropped from her nerveless fingers to the floor. Mrs. Kingsley picked it up eagerly, and in another instant cried out in a piteous tone:

"My God! and this is my work."

She was overwhelmed by torture and remorse, and, wringing her hands in bitter agony, walked the floor in utter despair. The cup of her folly she had at last drained to its dregs.

And still the sun sent its soft, bright beams into the room and athwart the faces of these two, whose souls were enshrouded in densest gloom.

Hearing the pathetic cry from Mrs. Kingsley's lips, Marion, with an effort that was heroic, with a will that was supreme, forced the energy of action into her enfeebled limbs, and, flying to her mother, clasped her reassuringly in her arms.

At length this never to be forgotten day was drawing to a close. The midnight hour was close at hand. There was no sleep for Marion. The emotions of her soul precluded repose of brain. In the train of thought surging through her mind there came the recollection of that other letter—the one accompanying Derringforth's. It lay on her writing desk, and to get it was no small effort, exhausted as she was. But it was soon in her hands, and then she noticed what had not attracted her attention at first, that the envelope bore the official stamp of the government.

"This is strange," she murmured. Tearing it open she was startled at the sight of her own handwriting on a letter inclosed, addressed to Derringforth. She dropped it in momentary fright, as if some uncanny thing had crept into her hands. The next instant she picked it up, and examining the envelope saw that it had been opened and that it was an old traveler, having first been sent to Derringforth's office, then to Omaha, then to Dakota, then to Washington, and finally having come back to her. She felt a strange dread as she took it from the envelope —almost a superstitious dread. That this letter— some old forgotten letter of hers, should come back to her, accompanying the announcement of Phil's engagement, was a coincidence so strange, so unaccountable, that she shrank from reading her own words, and lay for some moments with her eyes fixed upon the ceiling in a tumult of emotions.

Then with trembling fingers she held up the dainty paper and beheld the letter that Phil had never answered.

"This is cruel—oh, the cruelty of fate!" she sobbed. "But for this it would have been different. *Now* it is too late. He is lost to me, and life—my life, is without one spark of hope."

LVII.

GREAT banks of fog hung over the city. The morning was as cheerless as Marion's soul. Her mother, weighed down by the torture of remorse, had not yet been able to find the strength to leave her room. Marion was alone. It had called forth all the powers of her will to drag herself from her bed.

"But I must bear up," she murmured. "I must not give way like a weak child."

She looked up at the clock with a shudder. The hands were nearing that fateful hour which yesterday had dealt her a blow crueler than death itself.

A strange, almost prophetic dread seized her. Would the postman pass her by, or would he bring her yet other messengers of woe? A shrill whistle pierced the stillness of her room. Marion's fingers involuntarily tightened their grip upon the arms of the chair. A moment later her maid appeared at the door. She held in her hand two letters. Marion saw them, and her heart almost stopped beating.

"Two more letters!" she exclaimed under her breath. She took them with something of superstitious awe. The maid had gone, and Marion had not yet summoned the courage to look at them. She turned her eyes toward the window. The air was filled with a flurry of snow. She instinctively drew the shawl more closely about her.

"But whatever tidings of sorrow these letters may contain," she reflected, "it cannot be so bitter as yesterday's."

One was from across the Atlantic; the other from the shores of the Pacific. She recognized the writing on the latter and opened it first. It began:

DEAR MARION:
I am the happiest fellow in the world, and I want to tell you all about it. I am engaged. She is a Boston girl. Eleanor is her name. Isn't it a jolly, sweet name—Eleanor Donaldson, but the last name doesn't count, as she will soon change that. I met her in the oddest way. You know, I left New York early the next morning after saying good night to you at the dance. You must have thought me insane to come away so abruptly, but it was fate, dead sure.

Then followed an exuberant account of the somewhat romantic meeting on the train. Continuing the story, he gave glimpses of the halcyon days he and Eleanor passed together at Santa Barbara, and the yet more enchanting weeks at the ranch.

When Marion had finished reading this letter the hand that held it dropped nervelessly to her lap, and she sat motionless and looked long into vacancy. Then, with a sigh, she picked up the other letter.

She was not quite sure of the writer. She opened it and turned to the signature. "Harriet Devonshire," she read. The letter ran as follows:

My Dear Marion :

It is almost more than I can do to write to you at this time, but it was his last request that I should do so. Richard was buried yesterday. It is too much : too awful to realize. His death came almost without warning. He was out riding when a vicious runaway horse dashed around a bend in the road and collided with him. Both horses were thrown, carrying my brother down with them. He was insensible when picked up and taken to the hospital. We were notified of the accident and went to him at once. Before he died he regained consciousness, and, realizing that he had but a few moments to live, he said :

"Tell Marion that my last thoughts are of her. May God give her all the happiness she deserves. I loved her as I loved my life." These were his last words. His eyes closed, and very soon his terrible suffering was over.

Oh, Marion, it is so cruel—so hard for us. The sorrow is greater than we can bear.

These tidings pierced Marion's heart, and the tears blinded her eyes. She was in the presence of death. A friend had been taken from her—his life crushed out in a flash, and the last earthly message of that life was to her—the last solicitude of that heart was for her.

"Oh, this world of sorrow," she moaned ; "this cruel, cruel world !"

LVIII.

DERRINGFORTH never dodged a responsibility. There was a rugged honesty in his nature that made him see in a straight line and act on that line. He possessed those qualities that make the hero on the field of battle. He had gone so far with Dorothy that he could not honorably turn back. He had stretched out his hand to her when his soul was starving. She took it with childlike faith, and gave him all the love of her young life. The longing of his heart was stilled, and he was happy. But one day fate brought him and Marion together again, and in a breath that old deep love that had been forced into subjection, bounded up, and with resistless power swayed him from the later love. Duty and obligation, however, pointed but one way, and Derringforth followed in that way, steeling himself against all the protests of his heart.

To write Marion what he had done was something that called for all the courage he possessed.

"But she must know of my engagement," he reflected—"must know of it from me."

Five days had passed and Derringforth had received

no response to his letter. And what days of suspense! Why had she ignored him? A thousand fancies surged through his brain, some awakening bitter feelings, others paling his cheeks with dread. Oh, was ever time so sluggish?—and this, too, just when it should have sped as the fleeting gleam of a radiant sunbeam.

But at last Marion's letter came, and Derringforth seized it with the eagerness of one whose very life depended upon the message it bore. A sudden light broke upon his face as he saw his name once more in her own hand, and a look came into his eyes that, had Dorothy seen it, would have driven all the youth and joy out of her young life.

Derringforth tilted the letter up mechanically as if to tear it open with his finger. Then he stopped suddenly, and taking his knife from his pocket opened the keen small blade. With this he slit the envelope almost tenderly. In his eyes even it was sacred. His hands trembled as he drew out the letter and unfolded it. Now that it had come he dreaded reading it. Had Marion censured him, or was his engagement a matter of such indifference to her that she had finally sent him a merely conventional note of meaningless congratulations? This last thought froze the very action of his heart. He would a thousand times rather be condemned in bitterest language than feel that he was no more to her than one of the shifting pebbles upon the beach.

"I can defend myself if she censures me," he reflected: "I could not do otherwise than I have done."

Here is Marion's letter:

DEAR PHIL:

It was very good of you to think of me first in the dawn of your happiness, and to wish me to know in advance of all others of your good fortune. I appreciate this, Phil, and thank you sincerely—with that same sincerity with which I congratulate you on your engagement to so sweet a girl as Miss Rayburn. Though I cannot claim her acquaintance, I know her father and mother very well. They are delightful people, and all I know of Miss Rayburn pictures her as a charming girl, young and very pretty. You are a fortunate boy, Phil, and I wish you all the joy that should be yours—that will be yours. And may this same happiness, in equal measure, come to her who is to be your wife. It could hardly be otherwise, with you, Phil, as her husband.

I thank you, too, for wishing that your fiancée and myself may become close friends. I shall be glad to meet her and to know her as you desire. But not quite yet. I am hardly strong enough. I have been very seriously ill, and am still almost helplessly weak, as you may well judge from the appearance of my writing.

Sincerely your friend,
MARION KINGSLEY.

Tuesday, the thirteenth.

There were tears in Derringforth's eyes when he had finished reading this letter, and he walked the floor silently.

Marion had tried to write a reply that would breathe of good fellowship—a cordial, friendly note in which there would be nothing to suggest the utter gloom of her life. "Phil must never know," she murmured as she wrote, and her letter bore on its face no sign of the struggle it had cost her. There was no trace of the burning tears that dimmed her eyes; no evidence of the cruel blow he had dealt her.

But heart interprets heart, when both are alike attuned.

Derringforth saw beneath the written words and read there the story of her love, and beheld a soul from which all the light and hope had been stricken by his own hand. In the very dawn of this revelation a thrill of sweetest joy sent the warm, red blood bounding to Derringforth's cheeks, but in another instant he staggered, stunned by all he had seen in this flash of light.

"This is too much!" he cried under his breath, turning his eyes toward heaven. "And I am powerless!"

Oh, the pathos; the unutterable sadness of that cry!

LIX.

IT was June.

A thousand eyes followed Dorothy as she walked up the aisle on her father's arm; a thousand hearts burst forth into an exclamation of delight. There was youth and sweetness and love in her face. Few brides have looked happier than Dorothy; few men have looked more manly than Derringforth as he met her at the altar.

Marion was not of the friends gathered to witness this scene. She was spared the ordeal—an ordeal that perchance she could not have borne. Her somber garments, the outward expression of a sorrow scarcely less poignant, saved her from this supreme test of her endurance. The first throb of grief awakened by her mother's death had scarcely yet been stilled.

"And this is Phil's wedding day," she murmured, looking up at the tiny clock on her mantel. "Only a half hour more," she faltered, and with a stifled sigh that cried to heaven she stepped to the window and looked out upon the soft summer day. The sunshine, in contrast with the somberness of her soul, was never so bright, and this very brightness made her shudder and turn away.

She walked the floor with bowed head—bent by a weight of sorrow that had well nigh crushed out all the hope of her life. The clock ticked on, keeping time with Marion's measured tread. She watched the hands as they crawled toward the fateful hour—watched them with that same dread that fascinates him whose doom is but a span ahead.

And now she stopped again at the window, and her eyes fell upon a group of children at their merry games in the street. *There* was happiness, and a little way down the avenue was another scene of happiness. Carriages bearing guests to the wedding—Phil's wedding—were already rolling past. Marion's hand pressed hard against her heart. As she stood there she saw Phil looking toward the house as he had done on that memorable night when a word from her would have brought him back and made them one again. And this word was spoken—spoken too late—spoken when he had gone beyond the sound of her voice, and even now he did not know that her heart had yearned to recall him.

The vividness of that scene came back to her with overwhelming force. A whisper of tenderness from either would have melted the heart of the other, and the frigid atmosphere that chilled them into coldness would have become as the soft sunshine of a summer day.

Lost for a time in this reverie she was dead to the passing of the precious moments. Recalled to herself, she turned quickly to the clock. It still lacked five minutes of the hour. With a tread that was pathetic she again paced the floor. Her face was deathly white. Her left hand was still pressed to her heart, and in her right she held a handkerchief with which she dried the tears that ever and anon stole down her cheek. And still the moments sped and each tick of the clock was a fresh stab in Marion's heart.

"Two minutes more," she murmured; "two minutes, and Phil will be lost to me forever. Oh, God, must this be?" she moaned, lifting her eyes toward heaven. "It is not right," she pleaded, "not right. I cannot think I deserve this fate—this worse than death."

She reeled as if about to fall. She cast her eyes entreatingly toward the clock, and at that very instant the first stroke of the dread hour sounded. She threw her hands above her head with a gesture of despair, and sank upon her couch.

There was another wedding on this same day. It was solemnized in Boston, where solemnizing is a fine art. The groom was Burton Edwards; the bride Eleanor Donaldson. Two bachelors were made benedicts; two girls were made happy. This way of putting it is perhaps misleading so far as concerns Burton Edwards; unless indeed the words "happiness" and "benedict" are synonymous. If they be, then the term as completely misrepresents Derringforth as the converse would misrepresent Edwards.

To expect Derringforth to be happy in the fullest sense, loving another with a finer and deeper love than that with which he loved his bride, would be to expect the impossible of the human heart. But Edwards, on the other hand, the measure of whose love for his bride was boundless, was happy as only a great boyish, buoyant nature can be happy. His confidence in himself—in his love for Eleanor—was as broad and deep as the sea. There was no cloud of distrust in his heavens, as there was in Derringforth's, to obscure the brightness of his wedding day.

And this delight, this enthusiasm, this abounding joy, was imparted to Eleanor. Indeed, it radiated from Edwards as do the beams from the rising sun, and all who came in contact with him felt its exhilarating influence.

But Eleanor was not more happy than Dorothy, though the latter's soul was not thrilled by this surcharged enthusiasm. Indeed, it did not need to be. It could hold no more. There is a supreme height beyond which no joy can carry one, and this height Dorothy had attained. In Derringforth, with no excess of feeling, no transitory flight of sentimental fancy—nothing but the stanchness of his character, the fineness of his fiber, the delicacy of his attentions —in him—her husband—Dorothy found the source of supremest joy. The linking of her heart with his

—the oneness of their lives—met the deepest and truest cravings of her soul.

She knew nothing of the repressed fire that was burning within his breast. He was enabled by the indomitable force of his will—by constant watchfulness over his every act, every word, every look—to keep this secret from her.

When Derringforth asked her to be his wife Dorothy had that confidence in him which at once dispelled all jealousy of Marion. She was too happy, too wise, to make herself miserable over the past. What if Derringforth had loved Marion, did he not now come to her—come of his own choice? And was not this sufficient proof of his love—ample assurance of his preference for the heart he would join to his own for life?

LX.

DERRINGFORTH had made money very fast since the resumption following his failure. His stroke had all the boldness that had hitherto characterized it. There was an impetuosity and force in the way he went at things that captured the admiration of the Street, and at the same time caused many to predict a second disaster.

But Derringforth's mind was not groveling on the earth with these little souls. It was reaching out where they could not follow him. If they could have seen its inner workings they would have discovered a purpose that did not appear on the surface. This became apparent from the many large deals in which he took active part, and through many of the telling onslaughts he made upon his enemies—onslaughts that came about in so indirect a way, but with such force, that they little realized his hand had struck the blow until they felt the bitter smart.

Burrock, led by Van Stump, and relying upon the multimillionaire's ability to down Derringforth again, was among the first to go down himself. And the

Street, knowing of his base treachery to Derringforth, had no words of sympathy for him in the hour of his disaster. Men of Burrock's type have little chance of regaining their footing there when once misfortune overtakes them. There is no place in the world where honor among men stands at a higher premium than in Wall Street. Whenever one whose dealings have been beyond suspicion is forced to the wall, a hundred helping hands are stretched out to him.

Burrock's luck, as is usually the case with such men, deserted him in the hour of his sorest need. Baffled on every hand, he turned to Van Stump for aid, but this worthy capitalist was deaf to his appeals, and Burrock, bankrupt and friendless, went like a cringing cur to Derringforth, the man he had conspired to ruin.

This was an hour of triumph for Derringforth, but the succor he gave was given as from a large soul that scorned to gloat over an enemy's downfall.

But his greatest triumph was yet to come. Van Stump had been maddened so many times by his failure to cope with Derringforth, that at length an implacable ferocity possessed him with a determination to ruin Derringforth again. But he was working against odds. His millions and all the subtle cunning of his nature were no match for Derringforth's brains.

Van Stump had elaborated a scheme that involved millions. It was known to him, as to all others, in fact, that Derringforth was dealing heavily in Lackawanna. This had been his pet stock almost from the day he entered Wall Street, and his name was closely identified with it. Van Stump chose this security for the battle ground. Derringforth had been buying heavily, and was carrying a load that few men would have dared to shoulder. But he had faith in the road, and was, in this instance as always, ready to back his judgment unreservedly.

Van Stump began his attack by depressing this stock two points at a single blow. The onslaught came when Derringforth had little expected a decline, and the depression caused his holdings to stand him a loss of nearly half a million dollars.

Elated by the success of his efforts thus far, and feeling that Derringforth could not hold out against this *coup*, Van Stump kept on hammering the stock with redoubled ferocity.

Derringforth grasped the situation instantaneously. There was not a moment to be lost. The combination against him was too strong to be resisted. Superb generalship alone could save him. In an instant his course was determined. He gave secret orders to sell, and at the same moment rushed to the Exchange and personally tried to sustain the stock by buying large blocks.

His presence—his bold effort to check the break and hold Lackawanna from going to pieces, caused the price to advance a point with a suddenness that astounded Van Stump and his crowd. But with a recklessness born of desperation, they threw great blocks upon the market, and Lackawanna broke half a dozen points in as many minutes.

This was exactly what Derringforth wanted. Operators lost their heads, and down, down went Lackawanna, Derringforth all the while buying, buying, and charging brokers with madness in allowing such a stock to be slaughtered. But for every share of stock he bought he secretly sold many more through his brokers, until his orders to sell suddenly ceased, and then they began buying for his account on so large a scale that like magic Lackawanna went bounding up. Operators who a few moments before were frantic to unload, were now equally frantic to save themselves, and, with a mighty rush, the stock went up, up, up, reaching in ten minutes a higher point than when Van Stump began his onslaught.

All this time Van Stump had been trying to hold the price down instead of buying to save himself, as Derringforth and others had done. The result of this half hour's struggle was that Van Stump, the millionaire, was the bankrupt, and Derringforth, the bankrupt, was the millionaire.

LXI.

WHILE Dorothy was in the country, enjoying the cool mountain breezes, Derringforth bought a handsome new house in New York, and having decorated and furnished it to his fancy, was enabled to give her a delightful surprise on her return to town in the fall. This was only one instance of his constant striving for her happiness.

Eleanor inclined toward living in Boston; Edwards favored the West. After a good deal of discussion they finally compromised on New York, a town broad enough to embrace both Boston and the West. And on second thought Eleanor was glad that the metropolis had been fixed upon, for now she and Dorothy could be so much together. Fortunately they secured a house in the same block with the Derringforths, and simultaneously these two girl friends began the womanly task of making homes for their husbands—homes in all that renders them charming and sweet.

In this kingdom all his own—this delightful paradise where wealth and refinement met the eye at every turn, and with Dorothy's sunny presence—her love and devotion—aye, her very worship, Derringforth could not well help enjoying a measure of happiness. No day passed that Dorothy's eyes did not sparkle with delight at some new evidence of her husband's untiring thoughtfulness for her pleasure; no night came that did not find him in full dress, thus paying that delicate compliment to her that so appeals to the soul of a refined woman. There was no evening that found him too tired to go with her to the play, or to escort her to some social function—to call on friends with her, or take her to Delmonico's for a dainty supper.

Was ever husband more devoted? Was ever girl wife more happy? Viewed as the world viewed it, they were an ideal couple; viewed as Dorothy viewed it, no husband and wife ever loved each other so much.

"Burton doesn't love Eleanor as Phil does me," she often reflected. "If he did he would not leave her so much alone."

But Edwards did love Eleanor. He had been married nearly eight months. Enthusiasm rarely reaches over such a space. Once he came back unexpectedly after starting for his club for the evening. He found Eleanor trying to hide the traces of tears.

"Why, Puss, what is this?—you are crying," he said, taking her up in his strong arms and kissing her in that impulsive, hearty way of his.

Eleanor tried very hard to choke back the sobs, but she could not, and in his arms she gave way and cried like a child.

"What does it mean, dear?" asked Edwards tenderly. "You are not happy—why did you not tell me before?"

"It isn't anything. I don't know what possessed me," answered Eleanor, throwing her white arms around her husband's neck and raising her lips to his.

"But it is something—you must tell me, little girl. It would kill me to think of you as unhappy. What has happened? Have you had bad news from home, or are you ill?"

Eleanor shook her head, and clung to him more closely. Edwards was puzzled. It did not for an instant occur to him that he could be at fault, for did he not love Eleanor with all his heart, and did she not know this? Certainly no man ever loved his wife more. He would willingly die for her, if need be, and she knew it.

No, it was something outside of himself. What could it be? Whom had Eleanor seen? No one but Dorothy, and Dorothy—no, she of all others could not have said anything to make Eleanor unhappy.

And with these reflections Edwards threw off his overcoat and called to the butler to ring for a messenger.

"Why, Burt, what are you going to do?" asked Eleanor, her heart bounding at the possibility of his remaining at home with her, though the likelihood of this seemed so remote that she dared not indulge even in the hope, knowing of his engagement at the club.

"Yes, little girl, I'm going to stay at home with you. I can't allow you to be unhappy."

"And you would make yourself miserable, dear, in trying to make me happy?"

"Miserable! What nonsense! I don't think it is fair, Puss, for you to say that. How could I be miserable with you?"

"Forgive me, dear. It isn't fair. I didn't mean it as you take it, but in a comparative sense only. I was thinking of your engagement with Dick, and the good time you two would have together."

"Why, what is Dick to me in comparison with my little wife?" And taking her two hands in his, he looked into her eyes in a way that amply atoned for the heartache his thoughtlessness had caused her.

"But, Burt, I mustn't allow you to stay at home. It is selfish in me, and Dick will be so disappointed."

"Oh, Dick will be all right. He won't mind. When he gets my telegram he will go off with the boys and have a good time."

"Go off with the boys and have a good time," repeated Eleanor to herself with rising inflection; and then, with a horrible fear that her husband had read her thoughts, she said quickly and with a scarcely perceptible blush, "You are the dearest boy in the world, Burt. How many men would so readily give up an evening's pleasure for their wives as you do for me?"

"Now, Puss, don't try to make me think that. I don't give you half the time I ought to. But you know I love you, and would sacrifice my life for you."

And so he would, but not his pleasure.

"I know you would, Burt, you generous soul. I'm afraid I ill deserve such devotion."

"You deserve far more, dear, than I give you. Now, if I were only more like Derringforth, I could make you happier; but you know my nature craves excitement and activity. I wasn't reared indoors. I grew up on a ranch, in the open air—in the saddle—and I must be on the move all the time; otherwise I am as a fish out of water."

"Do you think I should love you half so much if you were more like anybody but your own dear self?" returned Eleanor, looking up into his eyes convincingly.

"You do have the sweetest way of making me think myself perfection, when I know I am not; but somehow I just delight in having my eyes blinded."

Eleanor smiled exultantly. "But," she said, "if I could only do this half so cleverly as Dorothy does it with Phil, you would be even more delighted. Did you ever see such jolly chums as they are?"

"Never in my life, and the strangest part of it is that he should ever care for Dorothy so much when he was so utterly broken up over Marion Kingsley. I don't believe a fellow ever loved a girl more than he did her, and yet see how happy he is with Dorothy."

The evening slipped by all too quickly with Eleanor. The dreary hours of loneliness she had anticipated had unexpectedly been made bright with happiness. Love, with all its tender sweetness, was there.

The next night Edwards again generously remained at home, and Eleanor anticipated another evening of delight. But somehow it was not the same. Edwards tried very hard to appear contented; Eleanor put forth every effort to give to conversation something of the spirit of the night before. But it lacked that freshness without which it can never touch a responsive chord in the soul.

Finally Eleanor suggested cards. Edwards readily acquiesced, and made an unsuccessful feint at entering into the spirit of the game with hearty enjoyment. But how tame! Two handed euchre, and with a woman, in comparison with poker at the club, where the chips pile high!

At length the evening was gone, and Edwards gave a gasp of relief. But his resolution to make Eleanor happy had not yet entirely oozed away. So the next night they went to the play. Just as luck would have it, the piece proved to be a weak attempt at satire on society—the sort of thing that bored Edwards almost to distraction. Eleanor herself, realizing his feeling, was miserably unhappy, and, as on the previous day, ready to draw a sigh of relief when the evening was past.

Still again, on the following night, Edwards played the rôle of martyr, absenting himself from the world that attuned the chords of his nature to music. When dinner was over, and his cigar smoked, he looked appealingly to Eleanor for some suggestion to help him through the weary hours ahead.

"You are dreadfully bored, Burt," she said. "Why don't you run down to your club and see the boys? You are just dying to go—you are, aren't you? Now be honest!"

"What nonsense you talk, little girl," returned Edwards, trying very hard to keep his face straight.

"You know I'm not talking nonsense," laughed Eleanor, amused at his effort to appear serious.

"Then do I really look like a dying man?"

"Well, not exactly, but you look a very much bored man, and I'm going to protest. It isn't a bit flattering to me. You must either go to the club, or we shall have to go out somewhere. It won't do to keep you here."

"You are the sweetest little queen in the world," answered Edwards admiringly. "I can't disobey you; we will go somewhere—anywhere but to the theater."

"You really won't go to the club?"

"No, not tonight."

"Suppose, then, we run in and see the Derringforths for a little while?"

"Do you really want to go there?"

"I think we should enjoy it—don't you?"

There was a shrug of the shoulders. "Going there means a dress suit."

"Oh, not necessarily."

"Well, yes; Derringforth never fails to put on one."

"Would it be very much trouble for you to change?—it would only take you a few minutes."

"But it's a deuced nuisance—makes a man a lot of useless trouble. I don't see the sense in such agony, unless of course one is going out where such dress is demanded, and even then I think it foolish, many times. It's a foreign custom—nothing American about it. Up to within a year or two mighty few men in this country wasted their energy in this way, and even now, in the West, there is much less of such nonsense."

Eleanor's face lacked the expression of confirmation that Edwards desired to see. "Certainly we shouldn't feel obliged to dress elaborately to call on Dorothy and Phil."

Edwards seemingly didn't feel quite satisfied with the way Eleanor received his remarks. He got up and stood lazily in front of the mirror. Then he adjusted his coat, squared his shoulders, and stretched himself up to his full height.

"This don't look half bad, little Puss," he said, evidently rather proud of himself; and then he walked over to Eleanor, and like a great boy bent over her, swung his arms about her, and kissed her. "Don't you think I'm all right as I am, dear?" he asked. "I know you do—come on, let's go. I don't mind if Derringforth is dressed in royal robes. I like to see a man have a little individuality."

LXII.

DEATH is not always without some compensating features. That keen sorrow which plunged Marion into deeper gloom—the loss of her mother—like a gentle hand tenderly shielded her from mingling with the gay world when her heart was dead to its allurements.

It was this same world that was chiefly responsible for the wrecking of her life. She could not think of it without a shudder, and longed to get away from it and its very atmosphere. The summer was before her. It was an eternity, as she saw it, without one bright spot, one wave of sunlight, to bring warmth and cheer to her enshrouded soul.

"I wish we could go into the woods, papa," she said, "where you and I could be alone. I haven't the strength or the courage to mingle with people. I want to go where I can be away from every one but you. Wouldn't you like the woods—would you be very lonely? I should try to keep you from being very lonely."

"I am glad you have made this suggestion," replied the father, his face brightening. "I believe it will be the very best thing for you, and I should like it myself. You must know, my dear, that I should be contented if I could see your youth and health returning."

Marion looked up quickly into her father's face. The tears filled her eyes. She tried to speak, but the words choked in her throat. It was scarcely a week, yet, since Phil's wedding day.

The middle of June saw her wish realized. She was in the Maine woods, far up toward the Canadian line, and among the giant pines. The camp was in a small clearing on the edge of as picturesque a little lake as heart could desire. It was late at night when she arrived, and its beauty was veiled from her eyes. But even the darkness did not rob her first hours in the woods of the sweetest air she had ever breathed.

"What a perfect little gem!" she exclaimed; "and this is what you call a camp—it is the sweetest, snuggest little house I ever saw."

Mr. Kingsley was delighted. "Did you fancy I was bringing you to a rude log cabin?" he replied, adding, "just wait until morning, when you can see how really unique it is. It was designed by a young artist, who built it for himself without regard to cost, and then—just like an artist—soon wearied of his fad."

Marion slept that night as a child sleeps, and was awakened in the morning by the sweet music of the birds. The bright sunlight flooded her room, and she could hear the soft lapping of the waters on the beach, but a stone's throw from her window.

"How peaceful and soothing this is," she reflected. "I am so glad to be here;" and she raised her eyes to Heaven with grateful thanks.

Half an hour later she was on the piazza beside her father, and feasting her eyes on the beautiful sheet of water before her.

"Oh, papa, this *is* a new world!" she exclaimed, slipping her arm through his. "I have never seen anything so charming in all my life."

"It is one of God's beauty spots," returned the father, his heart gladdened by Marion's evident delight.

A moment's pause ensued, and then she answered, "Yes, one of God's beauty spots, and it is our privilege to enjoy it."

There was something so impressive in the way she said this that her father cast a quick glance of inquiry at her eyes.

"Do you know, papa," she went on, "this seems like God's world—not man's. How different the atmosphere! What harmony and sweetness everywhere! It is nature, the very heart of nature. Another week of New York, with its heat and dust and noise—with its sad and cruel memories—would have killed me. Oh, papa, you didn't know—you never can know—how I longed to get away from there. I felt that my endurance was almost gone; that whatever bravery I had been able to command was breaking up. But now that I am here in this new world, where everything is so peaceful and beautiful, I am sure I shall have the strength to prove myself a woman — such a woman as your daughter should be."

"My poor child," said the father, pressing his lips to her forehead, "you have been very brave. I have realized your suffering during these dark days, and my heart has ached for you."

It was indeed a life of seclusion that this father and daughter were entering upon, compared with that they had lived; but it was just the sort of life best suited to Marion in her present state of mind. She was incapable of deriving morbid pleasure from grief; of making a luxury of mourning, as too many do. There was blood in her veins. She could not shrink into the corner of her room, and there, in somber shadow, helplessly bemoan her fate, forgetting that God had given her youth and hands and brain.

But the uses to which these had been put for the last few years now palled upon her; and with that old sweet life of her girlhood she was no longer in touch. To get back to it was the cry of her heart.

Many a soul has echoed this cry in vain. To return *at a step*, as it were, from the scenes that dazzle and intoxicate the senses, to the quiet, restful halls of nature, hoping to find the same pleasures that thrilled the heart in the sweet old days, is to expect the impossible. As time is an important factor in the formation of one's tastes for the artificial life, so, too, time must enter largely into the reformation of one's tastes for the natural life.

The weaker nature, finding the old pleasures flat and insipid, speedily abandons the experiment, and hastily returns to the gay world, to which alone it is attuned. But Marion was not of this type. Her horizon had a broader scope. Nevertheless, it was the dread of the world she had just left, rather than the present love of that to which she had escaped, that made it possible even for her to be led back to the simpler, sweeter tastes of life.

If it be as difficult for a rich man to enter the kingdom of heaven as for a camel to pass through the eye of a needle, so likewise it is equally difficult for one whose very life depends upon the intoxicating stimulus of the social world to get back to a place where the simpler pleasures will again bring delight to the soul.

One day when Marion had been at the camp little more than a month, a letter came that gave added impetus to the present trend of her life. It quickened into memory an almost forgotten incident, and warmed her heart with a sense of happiness that she had thought never again to know.

The letter recorded the gratitude of an old man

whom she had taken from the cold wintry streets and placed in a comfortable home.

"I cannot go," he wrote, "without telling you once more of my gratitude for your great kindness to me. My home here has been all that an old man without family and friends about him could hope for. It has been peaceful and comfortable, and but for the lack of ties that bring sweetness to old age, would have made me happy indeed. I was a wanderer in the streets, without a friend to whom I could go for a kindly look or a bit of bread, when you sent for me, fed and clothed me, cheered me with kind words, and gave me a home. Oh, I cannot tell you the brightness of that hour! If heaven be half so bright, it will more than fulfil the cravings of the human heart; and if extending a kindly hand to them that falter by the way be the best mission of life, then God will see in you the highest type of womanhood. I thank you again, as I have thanked you a thousand times before."

This letter was accompanied by a brief note, saying that Marion's beneficiary had requested that it be forwarded to her after his death.

"And he is dead, poor old man," said Marion softly. "Dead, and no friend to follow him to the grave or to mourn his going. How alone an old man is without wife or child! I am so glad I did something toward making him comfortable. I wish I had done something to make him happy. He gives me more credit than I deserve. I could have done more for him than I did."

Finally Marion took up the letter again and read: "If extending a kindly hand to them that falter by the way be the best mission of life"—and here she stopped, and her head rested upon her hands and she thought.

Mr. Kingsley was more than gratified at the improvement the first month in the woods had made in Marion's health and spirits. She began to look a little like her old self. Her step had regained something of its elasticity, and her cheeks were once more tinged with color.

But he was keen sighted enough to see that she must have something more than boating and fishing and shooting to maintain a permanent interest in this new life. He accordingly surprised her one day by handing her a deed of the camp and a large tract of the surrounding property, embracing an area of about two miles square. This made her absolute mistress of the lake with its picturesque settings.

Marion was overwhelmed. "I cannot realize it, papa," she said, "cannot believe that all this beautiful place is mine. How can I ever thank you enough? Of all the spots in the world I have ever seen, I love this the most. You couldn't have done anything to please me so much."

"Your delight, Marion, amply repays me for the outlay; and now that it is all yours, show me the genius you have for converting it into a park that will be the envy of all the country round. You shall have all the money you may require for this purpose. But let me suggest that your first thought be directed to enlarging the camp itself."

LXIII.

Mr. Kingsley displayed great cleverness in the method he had fixed upon for awakening Marion's interest to the full extent of her active nature. She at once began planning for the enlargement of the camp and the laying out of the park. It was not long before an army of men were busy under her directions, and it filled Mr. Kingsley's heart with satisfaction to see the enthusiasm with which she went at her work.

"Verily, human nature is malleable," he smiled, as he watched the perfect working of his scheme. "It can almost always be bent to one's liking when the right means is chosen."

The summer was gone all too quickly for Marion. It had not proved the eternity she had dreaded. The cold weather had already come, but she was unwilling to relinquish the work that had given her so much pleasure, and the men were kept busy until the snow made further progress with the park impossible. But those employed on the reconstruction of the camp were still retained, and Marion was with them so much that they soon came to constitute a part of her new world. In them she saw honesty—human nature in its simplicity, and she liked it, even as she liked the winter sports of which she had hitherto known nothing.

There was an exhilaration in skating, coasting, or a tramp through the woods on snow shoes, gun in hand, that was a refreshing novelty. In these there were health and healthy sentiments. She no longer found her music a bore, or a book a wearisome pastime. She had all the while been getting back toward the heart of nature, and was already in sympathetic touch with it.

"The holidays will soon be here, Marion," remarked Mr. Kingsley one evening. They had just finished a game of chess, and were sitting dreamily watching the blazing logs in the great fireplace.

"Yes; just think, we have been here almost six months."

"And you are not tired of it yet?"

"No; not yet."

"Wouldn't you rather spend the holidays in New York?"

"They would make me very lonely there; here I can make them bright. Shall I tell you of a little scheme I have had in mind?"

"Certainly. What is it?"

"Well, it is just this. I want to make the jolliest Christmas that ever was, for these mechanics and their families, and for our servants, not forgetting poor old Jack. I couldn't think of leaving him out; and there may be one or two others I should wish to ask. Now what do you think of it?"

"Unique, to say the least."

"But how do you like it?" urged Marion anxiously.

"On the whole, I like it—that is, if you have thought it all out, and find it can be done."

"It can be done. I have thought it out."

"And the eating and sleeping—rather important points, you know."

"Yes."

"You know the size of these men's families, I suppose?"

"Oh, yes—not so large as you might think, and besides, children are what we want. Christmas isn't Christmas without them, you know."

"Yes, that is so, but——"

"But it is possible to overdo a good thing, you think. Well, just wait. I shall manage everything beautifully, and you shall have at least half your bed."

It was the night before Christmas, and all in the house was not as still as the traditional mouse, for the half dozen mechanics, with their wives and children, were there; also Jack, the guide, and a number of his cronies, like himself, wise in woodcraft, together with a generous quota of servants, making, with Marion and her father, the most unique company of thirty ever gathered under one roof in that wild retreat.

The merrymaking began with a jolly college song, which Marion gave with a spirit that set the pace for the evening. The applause made the rafters ring. There was a heartiness, a genuineness about this that both amused and delighted her. Nothing would do but she must repeat the song. One thing particularly impressed her as she sang, and that was the expression of one of her listeners—a young girl of perhaps fifteen. With the others it was largely the words that brought laughter to their faces, but with this one it was the music that stirred her soul. She drank in every note with an earnestness that aroused Marion's interest. When the song was finished there were tears in her eyes, and her slight frame trembled from the intensity of her emotions.

She was the daughter of Adam Remsen, the head carpenter. Her name was Elizabeth. Dressed in the quaint fashion of the country, there was yet in her manner and features the refinement of the city. She had never before heard the notes of a piano, and they set all her nerves tingling.

If the guests could have had their way, they would have made Marion furnish all the entertainment for the evening, but this was not in accordance with her plans.

"Christmas is children's day," she protested; "we must give them a chance."

And little Billy Dunn stood up in his chair and piped off a declamation with a self complacency that made him the envy of the other children. There was nothing that gave Billy so enlarged a conception of his diminutive size as speech making. As he sat down, there was a look on his face which said, "Did you ever hear anything like that in New York?"

"Billy says he is goin' to be a orator," said his mother, patting him on the head proudly.

"I am sure he is," returned Marion. "He speaks with the ease of a veteran already."

"Well, I've spoke a good lot," interposed the young Demosthenes. "'Tain't nothin' new to me."

Elizabeth now contributed her share to the entertainment by singing a simple little ballad. It was sweetly sung, revealing qualities of voice that amazed Marion. She insisted upon its being repeated, and this recognition by Marion of the talent of one of their number fairly astounded the others. Elizabeth — Adam Remsen's girl! And they looked at each other, seeming to say, "Well, what's coming next?"

But there were two who cast no such glances. They were Adam Remsen and his wife, in whose eyes there were tears of joy.

There were other declamations, and then Marion sang again, receiving the same hearty applause as before. Here Dan Brierly, one of Jack's cronies, thinking to be a little facetious, and considering it would be a good thing to have a little fun at Jack's expense, said :

"Now that the other boys hev had their say, we ought ter hev a speech from you, Jack. Ye're great at speech makin'."

There was a howl of delight at this suggestion. Jack turned red and wobbled uncomfortably in his chair. "Speech, speech, speech!" called out the men in stentorian tones, forgetting where they were, and the cry was taken up by the boys, with the exception of little Billy Dunn, who was impressed with the conviction that Dan Brierly would much better have called on him. "The idea of old Jack Brammersly making a speech!" he said to himself, contemptuously elevating his little pug nose.

"I ain't no man ter shirk when there's somethin' ter be done," began Jack, rising and stretching himself up to the height of six feet three ; " and it 'pears ter me there is somethin' ter be done, and that is ter say a word or two about all this kindness from Miss Marion and her father."

These utterances had scarcely left his lips when there followed a thundering round of applause, showing the most hearty approval of his sentiments.

"It 'pears ter me," went on Jack, "that it's jest as well ter hit straight out from the shoulder and say what's in yer heart ter say, as ter repeat, as these here youngsters hev been doin', the words of them old fellers that was writ for another age and ter hit another mark.

When it comes down ter repeatin', I ain't in it—I hain't got no time fer repeatin' things, any way. And I ain't no orator, and I don't see why a man has got ter be ter say anything, if he has it ter say, and I hev somethin' ter say, and that is that nobody has ever come inter these woods that has brought in here anything like the square inches of big heartedness and liberalness that Miss Marion and her father has brought '' (ringing applause). " I tell yer what it is, and I know what I'm a talkin' about; there has been more fair days sence her comin', six months ago, than there was in the six years before her comin'. Why, it's been like another world, and yer all know it. We've all been rich, jest rich, that's what it is. We hain't wanted anything but what it's come ter us, hev we? Yer hain't none of yer known of anybody hereabouts bein' sick and goin' without a doctor, and jest slathers of medicine, hev yer? No, not one of yer; and yer hain't known of nobody, either, whose crops has failed 'em, and they've gone hungry. Now this is somethin' that don't happen once in a lifetime. I never run agin' it before in my lifetime, and I never expected ter run agin it till I'd gone yonder into the clearin'. But this ain't all. Where is there anybody else on these trappin' grounds, or any other, that would do what Miss Marion is doin' fer us all here tonight? Why, it's onaccountable, and we ain't none of us any kin of hern; and d' yer know, she has jest been workin' on this thing fer nigh onter a month—makin', buyin', plannin', and all this, and fer what?—not fer herself, I'll be bound, but fer us, jest ter give us a good time, and by the powerfulest buck I ever seed, ain't it a good time?—one that will keep our hearts young all the way ter the end of the trail."

Long before Jack's speech was finished all who had urged him to speak, thinking to have some rude fun at his expense, were gaping with wonder and amazement. He talked straight at them, his words carrying with the unerring aim of a bullet from his rifle. They understood him and agreed with him, and all stood up and cheered with hearty good will.

This simple, homely speech, from this great, strong man, took hold of Marion as no other speech had ever done. There was a rugged sincerity in his manner that gave eloquence to his utterance.

"I thank you, Jack, I thank you very much," she said, struggling to hide her emotion, and at the same time reached her hand out to him. He gave it that grasp that makes one instinctively say, "*he* is a man." And then, continuing, she added: "I have seen a good deal of polite life, and have met many men, both in this country and Europe. I have known many who could say very pretty things—who have said them to me; but none, Jack, not one, has ever paid me so fine a tribute as you have tonight."

Poor old Jack, he was embarrassed now, but nevertheless he was the hero of the hour, and good feeling ran riot through the hearts of all. Jack had always been regarded as an exceptionally tall man, but now, in the eyes of his friends, he seemed at least six feet taller than he was before, and they wondered that they had never recognized his true stature.

The Christmas tree had been rigged on wheels, and at this point it was pushed into the room, fairly groaning from its weight of treasures. How the eyes of young and old alike did sparkle, even as the gold and silver tinsel upon the tree! Not one of these country folk had ever seen such a sight before. Christmas had been a barren day with them—a day on which Santa Claus was supposed to do a good deal to help them make merry; but, as a matter of fact, he had done little or nothing. This year, however, through the charm of Marion's influence, he made ample amends, and showered gifts upon them until an intoxication of joy made the very room reel. Marion thought she had seen some pretty big eyes in children before, but never until tonight had she realized how big eyes really can be. Nor was the revelation communicated to her by the children alone.

The distribution of the presents was followed by a bountiful supper—a supper to be remembered by her guests throughout a lifetime. Marion was at a loss to know which gave her the keener delight, their gaping wonder over the Christmas tree, or their amazing capacity for the Christmas feast. After the supper half an hour of good old fashioned games, of the order of blind man's buff, brought the evening to a close, and a memorable evening it was.

But there was yet a good deal of fun for Marion in stowing away her guests for the night. Bright and early in the morning, the children, and those of older growth as well, were up and again delighting their hearts over their presents. After breakfast all became children together, and spent a merry Christmas morning out of doors, coasting on the glib white snow.

LXIV.

LATE in the afternoon of Christmas day, when all Marion's guests had gone, and she sat alone in the library, thinking over the pleasures of the last few hours, and watching through the window a stray snow bird flitting from branch to branch, the sound of sleigh bells suddenly fell upon her ear. A stranger was driving rapidly toward the house.

"What can it mean?" she thought. "What has happened?"

But the suspense was soon over. She held in her hand a small package bearing her name. The express messenger who brought it had come a distance of nearly twenty miles, making a special trip by the direction of the sender of the package. This fact, which Marion gleaned from the loquacious stranger, filled her with wonder, and she hurried to her own room to open it.

The removal of the wrapper revealed to her eyes a handsome seal leather case, on which her name was stamped in gold letters. Her heart beat faster. She unlocked the case, and there, nestling in folds of pale blue silk, was a tiny volume, perhaps three and a half inches long by two and a half wide. It was the most exquisite booklet eye had ever seen. The binding was made entirely of silver, bearing a chaste design, in the center of which was Marion's monogram.

She took it up with trembling fingers, and opening it, her eyes fell upon a card inclosed. One glance at the name, and all the passion of her heart—that old love that was her life—broke its chains and overpowered her. That name was Derringforth.

The leaves of the booklet were of heavy parchment, and on them was printed one of the beautiful songs of Tennyson's "Princess." There were no illustrations; nothing to mar the sweetness of the poem itself.

It was some time before Marion could calm herself sufficiently to open the covers again. When she did so, she read these lines:

> "Tears, idle tears, I know not what they mean,
> Tears from the depth of some divine despair
> Rise in the heart, and gather to the eyes,
> In looking on the happy autumn fields,
> And thinking of the days that are no more.
>
> "Fresh as the first beam glittering on a sail
> That brings our friends up from the under world;
> Sad as the last which reddens over one
> That sinks with all we love below the verge;
> So sad, so fresh, the days that are no more.

"Ah, sad and strange as in dark summer dawns
The earliest pipe of half awaken'd birds
To dying ears, when unto dying eyes
The casement slowly grows a glimmering square;
So sad, so strange, the days that are no more.

"Dear as remember'd kisses after death,
And sweet as those by hopeless fancy feign'd
On lips that are for others; deep as love,
Deep as first love, and wild with all regret;
O, Death in Life, the days that are no more!"

A ray of divine light came into Marion's eyes as she read these lines. They were not new to her, but beautiful as they were, she had never until now understood the depth of their meaning. She read them over and over. They were from Phil's own lips. He was with her, and, looking into her eyes, spoke from his very soul. Rarely has a wave of happiness so illumined a woman's face. The restraint of her will was overthrown for the moment, and the pent up passion of her heart swept on as a mountain torrent.

She pressed the booklet to her lips, and talked to it as if it were a thing of life. In each line of the monogram, and the design encircling it, she saw Phil's thought for her. *There* was tenderness, sympathy, delicacy, love. And the fact, too, that he had gone to the expense of sending a special messenger, so that this remembrance should arrive on Christmas day—all this meant so much to her. This hour with him—this hour of forgetfulness of all but him, this hour of abandon, of unrestrained joy—flooded her soul with the brightness of heaven.

"Oh, if it could only last," she sobbed. "If all the cruel past were to prove but a dream! But no. This little book says no. These walls, this park, this isolated life, all say no. Was it right in him, was it kind in him, to fan again into flame the stifled embers of my love? Was it right?" she repeated, an expression of despair dulling the eyes that but a few moments before shone with ecstatic light.

"Oh, the sweetness of this torture!" she cried, again pressing the little volume to her lips with the almost hysteric passion of the young mother clasping to her breast her dying babe.

"No, it was not wrong," she faltered. "Phil was not wrong, but oh, how cruel the reaction will be—how cruel it already begins to be. And yet if it were a thousand times harder to bear, I would rather bear it than not to have known the happiness of this hour—than not to know of Phil's thought for me. I can endure the gloom of my life with a braver heart, knowing what I now know. I did not expect this from him; I have not understood him until now. Oh, that I had; the bitter despair it would have saved me! To feel myself forgotten by him as I did —to feel that he never gave me a thought—did not know or care what had become of me—was the keenest torture of all. How I shall prize this tiny messenger from him! It was all he could do—perhaps more than he should have done; but if he has sinned against Dorothy, God will surely forgive him."

Upon this point Derringforth himself had taken much thought. He viewed it from every side—viewed it not in a narrow, conventional sense, but from a broad standpoint.

"It is not a question of technical sentimentality," he reasoned, "but one of the higher right. If it be wrong, this wrong to Dorothy would be less than the cruelty to Marion of forgetting that she lives at this holiday time. I cannot ask Dorothy to join me in sending her a remembrance. I would not hazard the chance of disturbing her happiness by even the suggestion. Neither can I allow this opportunity to pass without at least making the effort to cast a ray of brightness into Marion's isolated life. I cannot and will not forbear doing some little thing that will make her feel she is not forgotten by me—that the old days when our two lives were as one are still fresh in my memory. This little volume, bearing such assurance, will mean a good deal to her. I know it will. I wish for her sake, poor girl, it were not so."

But this thoughtfulness for Marion was not at Dorothy's expense. The ruling motive of Derringforth's life is well disclosed in his own words. "I would not hazard the chance of disturbing her happiness by even the suggestion."

Unlike Burton Edwards, his attentions had not flagged in the intervening months since his marriage.

Indeed, to do something—some little thing, perhaps —to make each day bright for Dorothy, had become the habit of his life. She had given her happiness into his keeping. He accepted the responsibility with a finer appreciation of all it meant than was shown by Burton Edwards—than is shown by most men, though they be far more in love with their wives than Derringforth was with Dorothy.

There was between them a delightful companionship, lacking which any union, however fervid the sentiment, is bound to be a disappointment. But beyond this solid foundation—this right foundation for the superstructure of a life partnership—there was a degree of love on Dorothy's part that was veritable worship. In her eyes Derringforth was perfect—a strong, manly man, and yet with the fine fiber of a girl. With him she was divinely happy. Her life was a perpetual summer—a rounded out perfection.

In such an atmosphere—hand in hand with such a companion—a wife so young, so sweet, so devoted— Derringforth could not fail to feel the fires of love within his own breast burn ever brighter and brighter. As time went on, and each grew to know the other better, to lean confidently, confidingly upon the other, their two natures blended into oneness. And the perfection, the complete rounding out of this oneness—the oneness of the family—the God touch —was given with the birth of their child.

LXV.

LITTLE Marjorie had just begun to be interesting. The long baby gowns had been displaced by the short frock. She was a mightily important personage in the Derringforth household. In the eyes of papa and mama she was indeed a wonder, and in her own bright eyes she was beginning to regard herself somewhat in this same light.

She had reached that eventful age when she could manage a well defined smile with marvelous effectiveness. And with what delight this smile was hailed by Derringforth and Dorothy! They had just spent half an hour in play with her, and reluctantly resigned her to the care of the nurse for the night. What a source of happiness she was to them! How big the place she filled in their world, and how bright she made it! She had attuned the sweetest and tenderest chords of their natures to harmony. The atmosphere of the family in its perfection pervaded their home — that atmosphere which the childless couple never knows.

When dinner was over they went to the library,

where they usually spent their evenings. It was a cozy, cheerful room, prettily decorated, and well stocked with books. A big, broad, leather covered, soft looking lounge, with great easy chairs to match, and a couple of tempting rockers, suggested rest and comfort. The furnishings throughout showed taste and a generous purse. In one corner of the room was a life size bronze, and in another was a unique writing desk. It was a present to Dorothy. Derringforth had had it made from a conception of his own, and at an extravagant cost. But it delighted Dorothy, and he was amply repaid for the outlay.

"I am glad we don't have to go out tonight," remarked Dorothy, bending over the library table and burying her face in a bunch of American Beauties. "How sweet!" she exclaimed. "You are the dearest boy to do so much for my happiness."

Derringforth had stopped in front of the grate, from which a soft wood fire sent a cheerful glow into the room.

"I am glad, too, that we are not going out, though I had planned to give you a jolly evening," returned Derringforth; "but I couldn't bring it about just right. I wonder if you have thought?" and he paused an instant.

"That we were married just a year and a half ago today," said Dorothy. "Yes, a woman always thinks of such things."

"And sometimes men," answered Derringforth.

Dorothy had joined him by the fire. He turned to her as he spoke, and taking her hand in his, slipped a marquise ring on her finger.

"Phil!" she exclaimed, her eyes dancing. "Oh, isn't it sweet, isn't it lovely?—the very thing I wanted so much!"

"Sometimes men do think," he repeated, enfolding her in his arms. She looked up into his face with tears of delight in her eyes. He kissed her fondly, saying, "This repays me a thousand times."

"I don't know how to thank you, Phil," murmured Dorothy, her head bent upon his breast.

"You don't need to put it into words. You have already thanked me eloquently with the delight that came into your face."

There was a moment's silence, and then Dorothy said, "I am so glad we didn't go out. I shouldn't have been half so happy. There is no place like our own dear home. You make it so bright for me—so sweet, so lovely, and how little I am able to do for you in return!"

"You do everything for me, dear. You have given me your life, your love—you are the mother of our child—the most devoted little wife in the world. What more could I expect? Why shouldn't I do everything to make you happy? I wish I had the genius to do more."

The rain dashed against the windows, and the cold November wind shrieked madly.

"Oh, what a wild night," exclaimed Dorothy.

Derringforth felt her frail frame shudder. She involuntarily stretched her hands out over the fire, as if to warm them.

"You are not cold, dear?" he said, stepping across the room to the thermometer. "Seventy two—about what I thought."

"It is the wind. How horribly shrill it sounds! It seems to blow right through me."

The light fell upon Dorothy's hands in a way that exaggerated their whiteness. Derringforth was startled at their pallor. He looked up quickly. Her face had a better color.

"This is the sweetest marquise I have ever seen," she said, bending over and examining it by the firelight. Then she stepped to the lamp to get a stronger light upon it. Derringforth went with her. That extreme pallor had vanished from her hands. He was puzzled.

"It was some trick of the lights and shadows," he reflected. "I shouldn't have allowed it to disturb me. It is silly to think about it."

"You have forgotten your cigar, Phil," said Dorothy. "What in the world does it mean?"

"Upon my soul I hadn't thought of it," laughed Derringforth. It was a forced laugh. That one instant had edged his anxiety.

"Let me fix you a light," said Dorothy, taking a bit of note paper from her desk and winding it into a well shaped taper. Then she lighted it from the fire. "Now, isn't this better than a ready made match?" she asked, applying the blaze to his cigar.

"A hundred times better," answered Derringforth. "You made it, that is why. This is a new brand. How do you like the flavor?" he went on, removing the cigar from his mouth, after a few vigorous puffs, and regarding it with interest.

"I was just going to ask about it. I noticed the difference in a minute—not so strong, is it?"

"No, not quite—a mighty well put together weed, though. By the way, I almost forgot—excuse me a minute and I'll bring them."

He was gone almost before the sentence was finished, and at the end of the minute returned with a bundle of papers—*Fliegende Blätter*, *Paris Illustré*, the London *Graphic*, and half a dozen other picture papers.

"*Fliegende Blätter* is particularly good this week," he said, pushing a large, comfortable chair up to the table for Dorothy. And then he took a seat on the arm beside her, and together they looked over the pictures, spending a pleasant half hour.

"I rather like this cigar," said Derringforth. "I believe I'll try another to make sure of the taste."

Dorothy laughed at his excuse, saying, "I must earn something to pay for all this extravagance." And she began busying herself with a bit of fancy work, while Derringforth lay back in his chair and puffed lazily at his cigar.

The storm increased in force, and whenever the wind shrieked fiercest he fancied he could see Dorothy shudder. She had not fully regained her accustomed vigor since the birth of little Marjorie. But never until tonight had he seen any cause for a moment's serious anxiety.

"And this cause tonight was a mere trick of the lights and shadows," he murmured.

But trick or otherwise, it had its effect on his mind. He tried to forget it. But that was not so easily done. He watched Dorothy as she worked, and his mind ran back to the year before, when her cheeks were rosy and round. The contrast was very great. He moved uneasily in his chair. The flavor of his cigar lost its sweetness.

"I don't like to see her affected so by the mere sound of the wind," he reflected. "If she were perfectly well, I don't believe it would disturb her so. This is all foolishness, I suppose," he went on, "but it is no easy matter to get rid of a thought of this kind, when for any reason, however trivial, it flashes into one's brain."

"I believe it is surely growing cold here, Phil," said Dorothy.

"I will put on some more wood," answered Derringforth. "Possibly the temperature is a trifle low."

He worked away at the fire until it burned briskly enough for a winter night. Then he looked at the thermometer. The mercury stood practically as before—barely a shade lower.

"How is it?" asked Dorothy, looking up as if expecting her impression to be verified.

"You are right," answered Derringforth. "The temperature has dropped—the wind must work through the windows. I shall have to have them looked over."

"I thought I couldn't be mistaken," said Dorothy, a smile accompanying her words.

Derringforth saw that it pleased her to find she was right. He had drawn the truth exceeding fine in indulging her in her fancy, and he was very glad he had not been unnecessarily accurate. "Little things mean so much to her," he said to himself— "the little bits of things."

His thoughts were interrupted by a sound that sent the cold chills scurrying over him. It was the slightest bit of a cough. He turned quickly to Dorothy, veiling his anxiety. "I am afraid you have taken cold," he said, fetching her a shawl.

"I don't think so. It is this bleak, cold wind— the very sound of it makes me shudder."

The sentence ended with another cough. It was so slight that ordinarily Derringforth would not have given it a thought; but now, with his sensibilities on a keen edge, it troubled him. He was not in the habit of worrying, but this was one of the times when he could not avoid it. He wanted to ask Dorothy about the cough, but he hesitated, fearing to disturb her.

"It may be that she has had it some time, and I have not noticed it," he told himself. "I dare say I should not have thought anything about it now, but for this trick of the firelight. In itself it is nothing—really nothing. For aught I know I may have quite as much cough myself."

But this reasoning did not allay his anxiety. His sleep was troubled. In the morning he went to Dorothy's physician and related his fears.

"I don't think you have the slightest cause for alarm," said the doctor. "The fact is you became startled, and then saw her through unnatural eyes. Why, haven't I seen her every week?"

"Yes, and so have I seen her every morning and every night," answered Derringforth. "If I had not been with her every day my eyes might have been opened before this."

"Nonsense, man. You must be ill yourself—let me see your tongue. You are the one that requires a physician's advice most, I fancy. Talk about being blind, why, if your eyes have been closed, so have mine."

"There isn't much to be gained from discussion," said Derringforth in his decisive way. "I wish you would see Dorothy this forenoon and then telephone me when I can see you. I will come up at any time."

"Very well," answered the doctor, adding, as

Derringforth got up to go, "don't let yourself worry any more. I assure you there is no occasion for it."

This advice was not so easily followed. It failed to quiet Derringforth's anxiety. He did little business during the forenoon. At one o'clock the looked for summons came. He hurried up town. There was a gravity in the doctor's expression that made Derringforth's heart sink.

"You have seen Dorothy?" he asked eagerly.

"Yes," answered the physician softly. "I made a very careful examination of her case. I wish I could tell you that your fears are groundless—that I was right in the opinion I expressed this morning. But I cannot. I found unmistakable evidences of pulmonary affection. I have seen nothing in her appearance hitherto to lead me to suspect such a trouble. She has had no cough. There have appeared none of the usual signs that foreshadow this disease. Your fears led me to investigate along another line. I was astounded to find that you were right. But the disease has made little headway. Now that we know what it is, I think we shall be able to combat it successfully."

LXVI.

"WHY, Phil, what has brought you home so early?" exclaimed Dorothy.

"I had to come up town, and it was so late I thought I wouldn't go back to the office," answered Derringforth, assuming all the carelessness he could command.

"I'm so glad you didn't. I wish you would steal more hours away from business."

"Do you know I have been thinking it wouldn't be a bad plan to sandwich in a little more leisure?" returned Derringforth.

"Why not do it?"

"It is not easily done, especially right in sight of my office."

"Oh, but you can manage it," said Dorothy persuasively.

"Possibly, but I have never yet made much of a success at it."

"You did beautifully the summer you were down home so long."

"I was a prisoner then, you know; and besides, I

was a couple of hundred miles away from my office. It isn't such a knack to loaf when a good big distance is between a man and his business. I fancy I could do it to perfection."

"Do let us go somewhere, then—anywhere you please—if it will only keep you from work," urged Dorothy.

"Do you really mean that?" asked Derringforth quickly.

"Certainly I do."

"I begin to feel that I do need a rest; but to be honest—real honest with you—I don't believe I could bring myself to the point of going. The market is very active just now."

"There is something in this world besides making money," returned Dorothy, adding, "now I am not going to allow you to back out."

"But I really didn't promise."

"But you will, now won't you?"

"You are not serious," protested Derringforth. "You wouldn't give up all these comforts for the sake of enforcing a rest upon me? And then there is Marjorie."

"Indeed I would. What are a few comforts to me compared to your health? And besides, money will buy comforts wherever we are."

"But how about Marjorie?"

"We can take her anywhere. Why not?"

"You shouldn't tempt me too much," said Derringforth in mock protest. "I might surprise you by saying yes."

"Why not surprise me now—this very minute?"

"Where should we go?" queried Derringforth.

"Where would you like to go?" asked Dorothy.

"I don't know. I haven't thought—almost anywhere, I suppose, where it is warm and sunny."

"Wouldn't it be delightful to get away from this cold winter?"

"It would indeed—say southern California, or down in Georgia, among the pines, where the air is sweet with balsam. I have always wanted to go there."

"So have I," answered Dorothy with increasing interest. "It must be very healthy. Oh, that reminds me—Dr. Barrows was here this morning."

"Was he?" returned Derringforth carelessly. "Marjorie isn't sick?"

"No; he said he was going by, and dropped in to see how we all were."

"That was very good of him, I am sure. Doctors are not usually so thoughtful. Barrows is a very decent fellow—a rather jolly man."

"Yes; he was awfully nice. He asked why I didn't get back my red cheeks—said he thought it was about time. It was a regular friendly call, but before he went he said he wanted to make sure how I am getting along, and so he took my temperature, listened to my heart, examined my lungs, and all that."

"I fancy it will be charged up in the bill," said Derringforth, aiming to disarm suspicion further.

"No; I don't believe it will. It wasn't a bit like a professional visit."

"Did he think you are getting back your strength as fast as he expected?"

"He didn't say, but seemed satisfied. But you are purposely getting away from the real question. I know you and your way of getting out of things."

"Afternoon teas, for instance," laughed Derringforth.

"Well, yes, but just now the point is, shall we go away?"

"To Georgia?"

"Yes, if you like."

"Here is my hand on it," said Derringforth.

Dorothy grasped it eagerly. How white and thin hers looked in his own!

"I am so glad," she said, fairly trembling with delight. "But I can hardly realize it."

"You may rely upon it, though. But there is one condition, and that is that we make quick work of getting away. You know when I make up my mind to do a thing I want to do it in a hurry. This is Wednesday. We can easily start by Saturday, I should think."

"Perhaps not easily, but we can get away. We could go tomorrow, as to that matter," answered Dorothy.

LXVII.

THE Derringforths had been at Thomasville a little more than six weeks. The new year had already dawned. The air was soft and balmy. The balsam of the pines gave it a delicious sweetness. Dorothy had gained steadily, as she saw herself, and yet she was not well; she was far from well. Just how this improvement could have been maintained for so many weeks without restoring her to her old time vigor is one of those problems that the normal mind cannot answer, but one to which the victim of pulmonary tuberculosis has almost invariably found a satisfactory solution.

But as Derringforth saw her Dorothy had undoubtedly lost ground since leaving home, and yet this failure from week to week had been so subtilely interspersed with improvement that even he was deceived as to the real gravity of her case. The slight cough, first noted on that night, mentioned in a previous chapter, had had an insidious growth. It was now master, and yet neither Dorothy nor Derringforth recognized its mastery.

Perhaps the assurance of Dr. Barrows went far towards blinding Derringforth's eyes, and this assurance was ably supplemented by the words of the Thomasville physician—a man of wide experience in the treatment of consumption. Dorothy was not the only sufferer from the dread disease who came before Derringforth's notice. There were hundreds of others, it seemed to him, who had come to that sunny region chasing the phantom of health. Each week brought its fresh quota of victims; each week ended the futile fight of some brave soul.

Many had spent their accumulated savings to reach this land where the atmosphere was laden with the balsam of life. Some had come through the charity of friends; others had been brought on the soft couches of wealth. As Derringforth looked upon these his heart was stirred to pity. "Poor souls," he murmured, with an ominous shake of the head. But in Dorothy's case he saw through the mist of hope.

At length he became impatient at the slow progress of her recovery, and one day, acting on the impulse of the moment, stepped into the telegraph office and summoned Dr. Barrows from New York, requesting that he bring with him a skilled specialist in pulmonary affections.

When the message had been flashed over the wires, Derringforth returned home to Dorothy. She lay on the couch. A smile of content came into her eyes as he entered. It was a summer-like day, with the temperature well up in the eighties, and yet she required the warmth of an afghan to make her comfortable.

Derringforth drew up a chair, and bending over her told her softly what he had just done. A look of startled inquiry flashed to her face. It was a struggle for Derringforth to maintain his composure.

"I don't believe Dr. Madigan understands you," he hastened to say, and, reaching over, took her hand within his own. In that warm, firm grasp there was reassurance for Dorothy. The expression of alarm gave place to confidence.

"I am glad Dr. Barrows is coming," she said, "though my cough is so much better that I really think we should not feel dissatisfied with Dr. Madigan."

"Yes, I know your cough is better, but I do not think you are gaining nearly so fast from his treatment as you should."

"You know you are always impatient, Phil," returned Dorothy.

"I dare say, but I want so much to see you well again. In this case I have good cause for impatience, don't you think so?"

"It will only be a little while," she answered, dropping her eyes, then quickly raising them to his, and adding hastily, "you know I am improving every day, and now that my cough is better I shall soon be my old self again."

That expression as her eyes dropped went straight to Derringforth's heart. Nerve himself as best he could, he felt his hands tremble as they clasped hers.

"But it will do you no harm to have Dr. Barrows come," he returned. "He always cheers you up, you know. I wish I had sent for him before. I should have done so, but Madigan has said right along that it often takes one a few weeks to get accustomed to the air, and that frequently the real benefits from the change are not apparent for some time."

"Ah, here is Marjorie," cried Dorothy eagerly. "Bring her here, Catherine," and she sat up and took her child in her arms. "You dear baby," she went on, kissing her rapturously, "mama treats you very badly to see so little of you."

"But mama gives baby more of her strength than she ought, now," said Derringforth. "You are getting to be a big girl for mama to hold;" and to Dorothy he added, "Let me take her; you will be completely tired out."

The mother yielded up her child reluctantly, but the little strength she had expended in these few happy minutes had been far too great a tax on her, and she lay back upon the pillow with a look of exhaustion.

LXVIII.

DR. BARROWS and his learned confrère had come and gone. Derringforth was in dense gloom. They had stripped his eyes of their illusion, and bade him see the inevitable.

"My God, must this be?" he cried from the depths of despair. "My wife, so young, so much to live for—the mother of our child. Oh, no, it cannot be, it shall not be!" And with the will of a strong, brave man he cried to death, "Stand back!" and placed himself between it and Dorothy.

"They say nothing can be done but to make her as comfortable as possible," he murmured. "I will not believe it; I will not stand idly by and see her life go from her, poor child. She is all courage. Her heart is as brave as a man's. If these doctors can do no more, she shall still be saved—saved by the power of will—by her will and by mine. We will throw their miserable drugs to the dogs," he cried bitterly, "and relying on God's help, and our own unfaltering hearts, we will fight back death."

And true to his words, he bent his whole soul to

this end. Never before had the full strength of this man, the entire reserve force of his nature, been aroused from its fullest depths. Hiding from Dorothy the cruel words of the doctors, he took her in his arms as if snatching her from the claws of the grim conqueror, and in this embrace he sought to impart from himself—from his own superabundant health—new life to her enfeebled frame.

And Dorothy responded to this soul infusion in a way that filled Derringforth's heart with renewed hope.

"You *are* gaining now, little girl, in a way that makes me happy," he told her, believing what he said, and saying what he did to stimulate her courage further.

"I am sure I am," returned Dorothy with a smile, "and if I had only leaned on you before, instead of these doctors, I should have been well long ago."

Derringforth watched over her tenderly, and waited on her day and night with untiring devotion—with a steadfastness of purpose in which his whole soul was centered. For a time, it seemed, he lifted her up by the very force of his will, infusing buoyancy and vigor into her wasted tissues. Her cough almost disappeared. The nights afforded her better rest. She was cheerful and hopeful, and talked of the future with the confidence of one in the perfection of health. Her plans for little Marjorie were gone into in detail. Derringforth said he would get a steam yacht for the summer, and they talked animatedly of the pleasures this would afford them.

But with this buoyancy of spirit there yet remained the stern fact that all the while her face became sharper, her hands more and more transparent.

"If I only had a better appetite," she said one day, "I should be all right now. Of course," she went on, "I can't gain strength very fast without eating, and there seems to be nothing down here that I relish. Sometimes I wish we were at home, but I suppose it is so cold in New York."

And yet Derringforth had drawn from the markets of the world to tempt her palate.

"When your mother comes she will prepare something for you that you will like," he said, adding, "she will be here tomorrow, you know."

"I shall be so glad to see her and papa," murmured Dorothy. "I wonder if mama can fix me something that will taste as it used to. How I would like to be as hungry as I was as a child in our old home."

"That same old appetite will come, dear," said Derringforth, "when we get on our yacht. There is no tonic like sea air."

Dorothy looked up with a sigh that seemed to cry to Derringforth, "Oh, but that is so far away!"

LXIX.

THE sweet perfume of flowers was borne in through the open windows, on the soft April air. Dorothy lay where she could look up into the blue sky. The music of the birds fell upon her ears, and she could hear the merry prattle of children at their play. She had got up at the usual hour, but her strength was now so far spent that she was soon forced to lie down again. Derringforth had just gone over to the hotel on an errand. Dorothy and her mother were alone. Presently her father came in with Marjorie in his arms.

"Bring baby here, papa," said Dorothy faintly, and she clasped her child to her bosom, her father still holding the little one.

Mrs. Rayburn turned away to hide the tears.

"I wish I could keep you with me, baby," said Dorothy in so low a tone that her words were scarcely audible, "but mama is so tired this morning," and she kissed the chubby little hands, and then her eyes closed as if from utter exhaustion.

A few minutes later Derringforth returned. Dorothy knew the step. It was music to her ears. Her eyes opened, and a smile such as he had never seen before lighted up her face. "I am so glad you have come," she whispered.

It was a moment that tested his powers to the uttermost to keep from breaking down before her.

"These are your favorites," he said tenderly, holding up a cluster of choice roses he had brought with him, and then placing them where she could inhale their sweetness. The word "lovely" hovered faintly on her lips, and she grasped his hand with sudden tightness and looked up at him. He bent his face to hers and kissed her. A light of contentment, of peace and happiness, came into her eyes. The vital spark had ceased to burn.

LXX.

THE Kingsleys' camp in the woods breathed of art. It was the conception of an artist. In this atmosphere Marion felt the artistic sense stirred in her own soul. Her brushes had lain idle since the day she was swung off into the social world. After that there had been no time for painting; no time for music and books. But now it was different—so different.

Thrown upon her own resources, she must do something to take her mind from herself and the dreary drag of time. There was no longer any Burton Edwards—any Devonshire—to pay her court; no longer any love from the man she loved. She was in a new world—an isolated world. The shadow of her sorrow made all about her gloomy. Idleness was death.

She turned to her brushes again as a refuge merely, but it was not long before she began to feel an interest in the work. It was work to her, for she applied herself seriously. But with equal seriousness she prosecuted the transformation of the park and the enlargement of the camp. The second season in the woods saw these two brought to an admirable state of perfection, and then in the early fall she went to Paris and placed herself under the instruction of one of the first artists of the French capital.

Her father was with her, and so, too, was the young girl who sang so sweetly on that Christmas night, now nearly a year ago. The quality of her voice and the refinement of her nature had at once awakened Marion's interest. Elizabeth spent a good deal of time at the camp thereafter, and Marion began lifting her to her own level.

Adam Remsen, Elizabeth's father, still plied the hammer and saw, but in his face there was a new light. Always a good mechanic, he was a better one now. He lived on a higher plane. His mind broke the fastenings of the narrow limits of his life, and in his management of the work on the camp he displayed an intelligence and an artistic feeling that amazed Marion. He was a bigger and abler man. Hope and pride had entered his breast.

But the full measure of his happiness was not reached until Marion told him of her purpose to take Elizabeth abroad with her, and educate her in music.

"She has a voice which, with proper training, will make her a great singer," said Marion, adding, "you will see Elizabeth famous, Mr. Remsen. She will bring great honor to your name."

Marion worked throughout the winter as few pupils are willing to work.

"Your application is wonderful, mademoiselle,"

said the old artist one day. "You have the feeling, the soul. I am proud of you."

These encouraging words from the great painter kindled Marion's ambition anew, and she worked harder than ever. But it was not very long after this that she received a letter from Burton Edwards which stunned her. It told of Derringforth's bereavement; of Dorothy's illness and death.

Oh, the whirl of emotions that rushed over her! She sank into a chair, and with cheeks white as marble pressed her hands to her forehead.

"Oh, Phil, Phil, how I pity you!" she cried. "My heart aches for you! And Dorothy dead—so young, so sweet, so much to live for! This life is such a mystery," she moaned. "What does it all mean?"

The tidings of Dorothy's death had come unheralded; had come with a suddenness that overwhelmed her. But the first wave of emotion had scarcely passed when a subtle thought flashed to her mind. "Now he is free," it whispered. Marion sprang up with horror. "Oh, that I should think of this in the very presence of death," she cried, her face flushing with a burning sense of guilt.

But the thought was not to be dislodged. It was nature asserting itself—the nature that had been wronged and trampled upon and crushed.

A little while later, when she had regained control of herself, she went to her desk and wrote to Derringforth:

DEAR PHIL :

This morning's mail brought me tidings that make my heart ache for you. I wish I could do something to comfort you—something that would make the gloom of your life a little less dense. But friendship can do no more than hold out a sustaining hand. How I wish I could do more—how I wish you could feel all the sympathy that goes out from my soul to you—how I wish she could know that my heart bleeds for her. It was cruel that she had to be taken. And she had so much to live for—so much to make her life bright and happy.

I had not even known of her illness until today. If I had, she would have received many messages of cheer from me. But these, I am sure, she did not miss, having you with her. My letter told me of the brave fight she made ; of the brave fight you made for her. The consciousness that you did everything that man could do to save her—the patience, the tenderness, the thoughtfulness with which you watched over her—all this will be a source of sweetest comfort to you.

If I were in New York, Phil, it might be then that I could give expression to a finer friendship than anything I can write will reveal to you. But I shall be there early in July, and that is not so far away.

As ever your friend,

PARIS, May 3d.   MARION.

Of all the words of condolence that reached Derringforth, these from Marion touched him deepest. " A sweet nature," he murmured ; " a true friend ; " and still holding her letter in his hand he cried over it like a girl.

A month had passed since that sad day in Georgia when Dorothy's young life went out. Derringforth had come back to New York, and was again in the Street. This is what he said of himself:

DEAR MARION:

No letter from you was ever more welcome than this one that reached me today. I know now what friendship such as yours means. Its sustaining influence is all, it seems to me, that keeps me up. My life has been wrenched from its moorings, and is going to pieces on the beach.

After it was all over I came back to the Street, hoping that by hard work I might, to some degree, divert my thoughts; but the hope was an illusion. My stroke had lost its force. All the vigor of my old life was gone. I barely had the energy to go to my office, much less to battle with the market. I still go down town nearly every day; but do not remain long. My strength is slipping from me; my grasp upon life is giving way.

There is only so much resistance in a man. The strain upon me during the last few months has well nigh exhausted it all.

This letter, I fancy, will surprise you, Marion. You have never seen me in such a mood, but I am no longer my old self. You say you will be here early in July. I shall be more than glad to see you. My friends are kindness itself, but it is the friendship between you and me, Marion, that runs back farthest.

As ever,

PHIL.

NEW YORK, May 14th.

The letter from Burton Edwards telling of Dorothy's death stunned Marion; this one from Derringforth reached a deeper chord.

"Oh, Phil," she cried, the tears streaming down her cheeks, "can this be you—you who were always so strong and brave? I cannot realize it. It must not be," and she walked the floor, all the anxiety of her soul aflame.

"Papa," she said, when her father came in a few moments after, "we must go home at once," and she handed Phil's letter to him.

LXXI.

As Marion was borne up the harbor on the great ocean racer, and saw the river craft plying hither and thither, she was forcibly reminded of that day when she saw Phil standing on the bow of the ferry boat.

"If he had only seen me as he looked into my eyes," she murmured, "it might have been different now. How straight and strong he was then! I can see him as distinctly as at that minute."

With this picture of youthful vigor—of stanch manliness—in her mind, she was brought face to face, a few hours later, with Derringforth himself. What a contrast! How pale and worn!

"I am so glad to see you," he said, grasping her hand with childlike eagerness. "I did not expect you until July, but I am glad you have come. And you, too, Mr. Kingsley."

"I thought you might need me, Phil," answered Marion, and she turned quickly away to hide her emotion.

Phil, scarcely less moved, staggered as he reached his hand to the table for support. There was a moment's silence, and then he said huskily: "Take this chair, Mr. Kingsley; and Marion, come and sit here on the lounge with me."

They were in the library, that same room in which Dorothy and Derringforth had been so happy.

No one felt like speaking. Marion dare not trust herself. She was beside Phil. His eyes were riveted upon the floor. Hers were still filled with repressed tears. Presently he turned abruptly to her, and with something of his old will power over himself commanded his trembling voice.

"When did you get in?" he asked.

There was a pause—and then Mr. Kingsley answered for Marion. "It was about two o'clock."

"And you have come to see me so soon?" returned Derringforth, a faint smile on his lips. "I appreciate this more than you can ever know. I am not quite my old self, and when a fellow is down he gets a bit gloomy, you know. But now you are here," and he raised his eyes instinctively to Marion, "I shall be brighter. It was so good of you to come home."

"A friendship that would have allowed me to remain away would be scarcely worth the having," answered Marion softly.

These words touched Phil. "I fear you have made too great a sacrifice."

"You can't believe that, Phil. I am sure you would sacrifice much more for me."

"You are the soul of generosity, Marion. Your

coming has done me good. I am a new man already. A few days of such improvement——" The sentence was broken by a harsh, hollow sounding cough.

Marion shuddered.

"A few days of such improvement," he repeated, "will make me myself again."

"It was this hope that brought us home," answered Marion, avoiding Phil's eyes. "I am sure we can do a good deal to cheer you up, and cheer is the best of medicine."

"This seems like old times, Marion," he answered with a smile.

"Yes, Phil," she faltered—for how unlike the old times to her—how unlike the rosy, round faced boy was the broken man beside her.

LXXII.

The warm June days began to tell on Derringforth. The noise of the city fretted him. He longed for the country, with its green fields, the rustle of leaves, the music of birds, the perfume of flowers, the refreshing breezes. He went down to the old home in Virginia. Everything there reminded him of Dorothy. The very atmosphere was oppressive. His gloom was intensified.

"I can't stand it," he said to Mrs. Rayburn at the end of the second day. "Every hour here, where I used to be so happy, is an eternity."

He took the night train for New York. The cool morning air sweeping across the Palisades and down the Hudson fanned his face as he crossed from the Jersey shore to the metropolis. He began to feel brighter. The shriek of whistles, the clang of bells, the grind of trucks, the swearing of drivers, were music to him—the rush and crowding of people, the eager faces, the nervous tremor of the town, were a stimulant. His spirits were on the rebound.

He went to his office and surprised his clerks, and

the friends he met in the Street, by the cheerfulness of his manner. He discussed the market, and talked confidently of his plans for the fall. Every one who saw him was encouraged by his hopefulness and evident improvement.

After a while he began to feel weary. The buoyancy was receding. He went home. He was very tired now, and realized that he had overtaxed his strength. He lay down and tried to sleep, but his cough troubled him more than ever before.

"I must have taken cold on the train," he said to himself, "and I was so much better."

He had been getting better for some time—in fact, ever since he wrote Marion that gloomy letter.

In the effort to save his wife he had given from his own vital force until there was little left. Then came the grief that crushed him. All was blackness. Every day he felt his strength slipping from him, and the end, it seemed to him, was not far off. But after a time a subtle change crept over him. The thought of death faded, and in its place came hope—at first barely a shadow, and then in its perfection.

Marion had taken advantage of Derringforth's absence, and had gone to the woods to look after things at the park. She was still there. He missed her. He had been leaning on her unconsciously. The stronger a man, the more helpless he often seems in sickness. The next day after his return from Virginia, he did not feel able to go down town. The hours dragged with him, and to add to his discomfort, the temperature rose to nearly a hundred. The heat exhausted him. The air was heavy with moisture. He slept little that night. In the morning the sun came up red with fierce heat. Derringforth was discouraged.

"I can't endure this another day," he murmured. "I must go somewhere."

With the thought of his experience in Virginia still fresh in his mind, he hesitated. But as the heat of the morning mounted higher and higher, he yielded and fled to the hills behind West Point. A cool breeze swept up through the valley, on either side of which was a picturesque range of mountains. Dotted along the plain were the homes of thrifty farmers, with gardens and fruit trees and green fields and pastures, with grazing cattle. On the rising slopes stood handsome cottages, the summer retreats of city people.

Derringforth sat on the veranda of the hotel, and viewed the scene before him. A thrill of admiration stirred his heart.

"This is beautiful," he exclaimed. "I am glad I am here."

But scenery cannot satisfy the human soul when it craves companionship. With the shadows of night settling in the valley, and creeping higher and higher up the mountain sides, there stole over Derringforth a sense of unutterable loneliness. His thoughts hovered over a fresh mound in a little cemetery in Virginia, and he longed to be beside her.

"There would be no more heartache," he murmured, "no more weariness, no more suffering."

And then little Marjorie came into his mind, and his face blanched.

"God forgive me," he cried with trembling lips. "I did not think—I must live for my child."

The next morning Derringforth took a drive, and came back refreshed but somewhat wearied. He threw himself into a large, comfortable rocker on the veranda. A number of people spoke to him on one pretext or another. There was a look of sympathy in their eyes; a note of sympathy in their tones. This was not what he wanted. It irritated him. He was not a sick man, and did not wish to be treated as such. Still he was civil to all, and to his regret, for they hung about him, and whenever he coughed their faces lengthened. This angered Derringforth.

"What fools!" he exclaimed petulantly. "I wish they would keep away. There is no companionship in them for me; none in the whole house. I wish I were in the wilderness."

Again the shadows of night fell upon the mountains, and their blackness loomed up into the dark heavens as a monster from the under world. Derringforth sat apart by himself. He had been watching the transformation.

"How lonely one can be in this world," he sighed,

"and nowhere so lonely as with people whose natures are not attuned to his."

A boy brought Derringforth's light overcoat. All the guests had come out from dinner, and were on the veranda. Most of them were thinly clad. When they saw Derringforth putting on his overcoat, they looked at him with a look that seemed to say, "Poor soul!"

A little old woman not far from him coughed and wiped away an imaginary tear. The cough was palpably one of sympathy.

"The night air settles down rather cold up here," remarked one of the acquaintances of the forenoon, mopping the perspiration from his ruddy face.

"My God!" exclaimed Derringforth under his breath, "I shall go mad if I don't get away from here. Between these people who look at me as if I were on the verge of the grave, and the loneliness of it all, I am about as miserable as one could be and live."

The next morning he went back to New York. Marion had not yet returned. Derringforth was disappointed, and yet he had no good reason for expecting her back so soon. She supposed he was still in Virginia.

But the next day she did come. She found Derringforth more depressed than she had yet seen him. He told her of the failure of his experiments in going out of town; of his fuming and fretting in town.

"The country is no longer the same," he went on. "The change can't all be with me, and yet—I wonder if it is—if the fields and the brooks and the birds, the frolics and the sports, mean as much to children now as they did to you and me, Marion?"

"I wonder if they do?" she answered, a far off look in her eyes.

"You have noticed the change, then?" he asked quickly.

"Yes, Phil. I have noticed the change." Her voice was low, almost sad. Then she added, "But there is a peacefulness and harmony in the woods that is restful to me."

Derringforth sighed softly. After a moment's silence he looked up. "Do you think I should find it restful there, Marion?" The words seemed to come from a weary, yearning soul.

"I think you would, Phil. I should like to have you try it."

"I should like to try it," he answered almost eagerly.

"I am so glad you suggested it," said Marion, a smile lighting up her face. "I have wanted to ask you before, but hesitated."

"I came near speaking about it before going to Virginia," returned Derringforth. "I have felt that it might be just the place for me, but like yourself I hesitated."

"But papa will be there. I cannot think your presence would shock good taste. The opinion of others at best is of small consequence to you, Phil, as compared with your health."

LXXIII.

"I AM beginning to feel the effect of this bracing air already," said Derringforth. "I am actually hungry."

"Are you truly?" returned Marion, her face brightening.

"I am, indeed."

"There is nothing like it anywhere," remarked Mr. Kingsley. "I never can eat enough up here."

"I hope it will be the same with you, Phil," said Marion.

They had been riding a couple of hours, and for the most part through the woods. The day was cool and invigorating. Presently they reached the summit of a hill, sometimes called a mountain. It afforded an extended view. The west was brilliant with golden yellow from the setting sun. A chain of lakes wound through the valley and nestled peacefully between the sloping banks. Here and there a clearing ran back from the water's edge—small farms with modest cottages and fields of waving grain. Giant pines, older than the traditions of the lakes, fanned the heavens, perfuming the air with delicious sweetness. The view burst suddenly upon Derringforth. He was speechless for a moment, and then his eyes met Marion's. "What a picture!" he exclaimed, his admiration stirred to its depths.

"I am so glad you like it, Phil," said Marion, delighted.

"It is beautiful—more beautiful than anything I have ever seen."

A quarter of an hour later they were in the park. The driver called to the horses. They responded with a rattling pace. The hard, smooth roads, winding in graceful curves, astonished Derringforth. The cool air was a tonic. He was in better spirits than for many a day. The road bent suddenly to the right, and the horses shot into a tiny clearing and up a graveled driveway to the camp. Derringforth's eyes were big with wonder. He stood on the veranda and looked at the lake. The red of the dying day was reflected on its smooth surface.

"Isn't it lovely?" said Marion, standing beside him.

"It is a gem," answered Derringforth, "and how beautiful the setting! I can understand already how you have found it restful here; I shall find it restful, too."

A sound overhead attracted Marion's attention. She looked up quickly. A flock of wild ducks was almost directly above them. Jack ran for a gun. He was back in an instant. It was in Marion's hands. Bang! bang! went both barrels in quick succession, and three fine birds swerved from their course, faltered, fluttered feebly, and fell.

"Splendid, splendid!" cried Derringforth, his nerves trembling with excitement. "I couldn't have done it myself."

"It's a part of the life up here," answered Marion, her cheeks flushed. "You will soon learn it—Jack will coach you as he did me."

LXXIV.

THE evening had not advanced far when that drowsy feeling, which usually possesses the fresh arrival in the woods, began to steal over Derringforth.

"I think I must say good night," he said to Marion, starting up suddenly. "I am very sleepy." But even now he lingered, the look in his eyes again saying a reluctant good night.

As he entered his room an expression of amazement flashed to his face. The feeling of drowsiness vanished. He was in a most unique bed chamber. The walls and ceiling had a subdued grayish tinge. They were made of young cedar trees, perhaps two inches in diameter, with the bark still on. Nothing could have given the apartment a more rustic appearance—a more woodsy flavor. The floor was covered with native skins—bear, otter, mink, and fox—while the walls were decorated with pictures of woodland scenes and antlered heads of deer and caribou. Half a dozen candles, screened by colored shades, shed a soft light over all.

The room faced the lake, with glass doors opening

on a tiny balcony. There was a connecting private bath, as modern in all respects as that of the city mansion—a porcelain tub, mosaic floor, and tiled walls.

The furniture had been made from special designs, and matched the ceiling in rustic quaintness. In everything Derringforth saw Marion's hand. The very atmosphere whispered softly of her. His heart awakened from its gloom, and for a moment he forgot himself and was happy. Then came a feeling of bitter penitence and shame.

"I ought not to have come here," he murmured.

Dorothy was with him now, and looking into her eyes his own filled with tears.

"My poor child," he moaned, "why were you ever taken from me?"

A wave of emotion swept over him. An impulse seized him. Obeying it, he staggered toward the lights and blew them out. All was inky darkness. He groped his way to a chair and sank into it. There was nothing now to remind him of Marion. He was alone with Dorothy. The deep shadows of the night could not hide her from his vision. He reached out his hands and drew her to him, and took her in his arms, just as he used to do. She looked up into his face just as she used to do, her soft blue eyes beaming with love. Her cheeks were as the roses; her breath as sweet as the dew. He pressed her to his breast and kissed her, and never was kiss more real— never did soul commune with soul as now.

"This is life again, dear," he whispered, "life to have you with me once more;" and his heart was as light as the air, and laughter was on his lips, and all the notes of joy and happiness of his soul gave forth sweet music.

But alas! the vision faded; the fancy fled. The rosy cheeks grew pale, the round, plump figure thin and wan, the light of the eye flickered feebly, and then death—cold, cruel death.

"Oh, God," he cried, lifting his eyes to heaven and starting up in agony. His head swam. The atmosphere had suddenly become heavy. He could barely breathe. He made his way across the room and opened the glass doors. He stepped out upon the little balcony and peered into the night.

The cool air fanned his face, and checked the faintness that had seized him. He looked at the lake, and then across to the black forest that fringed the further shore.

Just then a bright bit of gold caught his eye. His attention was instantly riveted. It was the moon, rising above the solid wall of giant trees. He watched it as it mounted higher and higher. All nature was as still as death. The lake was as peaceful as a sleeping child nestled in its mother's arms.

Presently the golden light was reflected on the water, and a shimmering path of moonbeams reached across to the shadow of the great pines. The scene awakened a feeling of awe in Derringforth. He fell into a train of reverie, from which he was ruthlessly aroused a few minutes later by a piercing scream that broke the stillness of the night, and went echoing through the forest. It was the screech of a night owl.

LXXV.

MARION tried to talk with her father after Phil had said good night, but the words would not come. In a little while she went to her room. She wished to be alone with her thoughts. She stood before her dressing case and looked at herself in the mirror. There were traces of anxiety in her face that she had not been able to hide. "I wonder if Phil sees?" and she bent closer to the glass. Then she turned away with a sigh, and stopping by the mantel rested her arm upon it. Her heart ached. Her head drooped.

"What a mistake it has all been," she murmured. "One false move, and two lives gone. Oh, why couldn't I have seen—why couldn't mama have seen? Phil did see, but I was blind. I thought nothing could come between us. How soon our lives began to drift apart! The channels widened day by day. Now they have suddenly come together again. But how different everything is!"

She turned back to the mirror and unloosed her hair. It fell about her face and over her shoulders, in soft, wavy masses. She was a young girl again. She went to her trunk and took out a handsome leather case. It contained Phil's photograph and the booklet he gave her. She pressed the likeness to her lips, and then, holding it a little way off, the tears filling her eyes, she exclaimed, " How changed, oh, how changed ! "

After a few moments she put down the photograph and took up the tiny volume. She opened it, and read and reread the song. It was in perfect harmony with her mood tonight. She threw herself wearily upon the couch, and with hands clasped across her eyes she repeated the poet's words :

> " Dear as remembered kisses after death,
> And sweet as those by hopeless fancy feign'd
> On lips that are for others ; deep as love,
> Deep as first love, and wild with all regret ;
> O, Death in Life, the days that are no more ! "

The strain on her had been very great. She still loved Derringforth with that same deep love, and yet she could not show it as in the old days. It must be concealed even from him. He was free and not free. It was harder for her now than when Dorothy stood between them. Then she absented herself from him. Now he was with her—in her very home.

Every week since her return from Paris he had been leaning more and more upon her. In her presence he found contentment ; away from her he was wretched. But this was not love. It did not satisfy a starving heart. And yet she would not have it otherwise. Her love for him was too pure, too unselfish, to wish him to look beyond the shadow of his fresh sorrow. Keen as was the pang of this starvation, it was more easily borne than her anxiety for him.

In the six weeks Marion had been at home Derringforth had surely failed. His strength was less, and his cough more racking. But the change had been gradual and deceptive. Sometimes Marion fancied she was mistaken; and hope made the world bright and sunny. Then a bad day, and he would drop back farther than before. She had talked with the doctor in New York. He was a straightforward man who believed in telling the truth. His face became very grave.

"It is a case of sacrifice," he said, "of heroism."

"What do you mean?" asked Marion quickly.

"I mean that in his efforts to save his wife, the treacherous disease that killed her fastened itself upon him."

"You can't mean this," cried Marion; "oh, don't, don't say it is fatal."

"There is always hope," returned the doctor, moved to sympathy. "Mr. Derringforth has an iron constitution and a marvelous will. But he must get away from New York. Bacteria thrive in this atmosphere. In a dry, pure air he might throw off the disease."

It was this statement that gave Marion hope. The air at the camp was all that could be desired, and now that Phil was to be there with her, her heart took courage. She remembered how she herself had gained, and she recalled the many accounts she had heard of the recovery of invalids who had gone there—some carried in on stretchers.

But this buoyancy of spirit had receded tonight. Perhaps the quiet of the woods had something to do with it. Possibly Phil's early good night disappointed her. It may be that a sense of misgiving had stolen over her. At all events she was gloomy. Hope had faded. She thought for a long time. The burden on her heart was like lead.

"I hope Phil will like the room," she reflected.

It had been designed and built for him. The pictures on the walls from her brush had been painted for him. In the purchase of the others his fancy had been consulted. The furniture was the result of long conversations with him. The bath room was added for his convenience. The soft bed and easy chairs were procured for his comfort. And all this, though she expected his eyes would never see the room and its belongings. Indeed, the whole camp had been remodeled and furnished according to his ideas. It was he, in fact, who laid out the park, she acting merely as his interpreter. And so it had been ever since that cruel wedding day. Her standard of life was gauged by his ideals. She lived in his approval, doing the things he would commend, avoiding the things he would dislike.

It was a strange return for all this, that he should plunge his room into darkness to shut out from his eyes all evidences of her. Could she have known what he did, as she lay there on the couch thinking of him—her heart bleeding for him, the gloom of that hour would have crushed her.

LXXVI.

It was August. The air of the hills was cool and bracing. Soft, fleecy clouds floated in the heavens, breaking the blue of the sky. A boat put out from the landing and skirted the shore of the lake, whose surface was like a polished mirror. Jack, the old guide, dipped the oars softly. The boat slipped gently through the water. Marion and Phil sat lazily in comfortable chairs, chatting carelessly, as if life ran on forever. They were in the shade of the tall pines.

"This comes mighty close to heaven," remarked Phil.

"It would be a pretty good heaven, wouldn't it?" answered Marion.

"I can't imagine anything more attractive. The conventional heaven with psalm tunes and languishing piety isn't in it with this."

"I'm afraid you are irreverent, Phil," returned Marion with a smile.

The sentence was barely finished when her reel flew around like mad. Her rod buckled sharply.

Her eyes sparkled. Her nerves tingled. The line paid out further and further. A merry fight was on.

"How he pulls," she cried excitedly, now winding in the line, now humoring the gamy trout. Presently the fish shot to the surface and leaped well out of water.

"Oh," she cried.

"It's a beauty," exclaimed Phil, scarcely less excited.

Fifteen minutes of the rarest sport followed, fifteen minutes of exhilarating, nerve tingling sport, and the trout, exhausted by the struggle, gave up the fight.

They had been out perhaps a couple of hours when they put in at a little cove. The result of the morning's fishing was a half dozen of as handsome trout as the lake had ever yielded up.

Now began preparations for a delicious meal. Marion and Phil sat on the trunk of a huge tree that had been leveled by the gale of the previous winter, their feet dangling aimlessly. They were as two children—idle, careless children. Phil had a handful of pebbles, and every now and then he tossed one into the lake. He and Marion watched the ripples as they spread out and out and were lost on the smooth surface of the water.

Jack made a primitive fireplace from the rocks on the beach. Then he gathered fine, dry wood, and built a blazing fire. Over this he placed a spider, in which there was a generous supply of salt pork.

While this was frying, he dressed the fish. Then he rolled them in corn meal, and they were ready for cooking.

"Begins to look appetizing already," remarked Phil.

Jack chuckled to himself.

"You will think you never ate trout before," answered Marion.

Jack removed the well fried slices of pork from the spider, and into the sizzling fat dropped the fish. Then he spread the cloth on a rude table he had constructed, and brought the dishes from the boat, together with the eatables from the camp. Every now and then he stopped to turn the fish and baste them.

Derringforth inhaled the savory odor. "By Jove!" he exclaimed, "I never did smell anything quite so good. See how crisp and brown they are getting," he went on, his appetite as keen as that of the small boy.

When the trout were done to a turn, and seasoned to the palate of an epicure, Jack took them from the spider, and into the remaining pork fat sliced a number of cold boiled potatoes. In a few minutes these were well browned. In the mean time he had prepared a pot of fragrant coffee, and now, with delight in his rugged face, he called Marion and Phil to the feast.

And it was a feast. The man who has never tasted

trout, cooked as a skilled guide can cook them, and served on the beach beside their native waters, does not know what trout are.

Derringforth ate as if he never was to have another meal. There was nothing about his appetite to suggest the invalid.

"A few more dinners like this, little girl, and I shall be as good as new," he laughed.

Marion's cheeks flushed. This was the first time he had called her by the old endearing term. He saw her heightened color, and felt his own cheeks burn.

The ice had been broken.

When they reached the camp a surprise was in waiting for Derringforth. He was in unusual spirits. He walked up from the boat with firm step, talking cheerily with Marion. He entered the camp and stopped as if stunned. There was little Marjorie.

He hesitated a moment, and then, with a cry of delight, flew to her and took her in his arms, and kissed her and talked to her with tears of joy in his eyes. Now Mrs. Rayburn came in, and there was a season of glad rejoicing. All this had been secretly arranged by Marion as a surprise for Phil.

LXXVII.

FROM now on Phil and Marion gravitated back toward childhood. Every day brought them a shade nearer to the old life. The atmosphere was softer; the world brighter. Impulse led them by the hand once more. Good fellowship—good chumship had returned.

The sun dipped into the northern sky, and summer was gone. Fall had come, and now Phil and Marion were children again in very truth. They had gone back—far back from that fatal day when misguided fancy decreed the ruin of their lives—back to that childhood which had been so bright and happy. They played the old games, and read the old books, and took the old tramps, in so far as Phil's impaired strength would permit. A crack at a squirrel, the snaring of a partridge, the winging of a hawk, a shot at a buck, brought back all the delights of a dozen years before.

The early fall went, and with it went childhood, and Phil and Marion were in young manhood and young womanhood. The horizon broadened, and they saw the world in a new light. It was beautiful. They looked into each other's eyes, and all this beauty was reflected there. They took each other's hands, and through that touch a current of love was flashed from heart to heart. The hills, and the lake, and the trees, whispered of love. The air was as the perfume of flowers; and the winds of heaven as soft, dreamy music. Over all, and in all, there was peace, and harmony, and rest.

And when the bleak storms of approaching winter came, they were as the gentle showers of spring to these two, who were back in the old days—the enchanting days of dawning love.

And thus Phil kept up, and gained, despite the disease that all the while had been digging deeper and deeper into his very life. But one day Marion was called to New York, and then the break came. She was away less than a week, but time enough for Phil to learn what her presence meant to him—time enough for him to see himself. He had been getting well steadily. He had not thought of dying. The revelation came suddenly. He clung to little Marjorie in a way that was pathetic.

" Papa goin' to cry," she said to him, looking up into his face. It was unutterably sad. The tears filled his eyes. He could not speak, but bent forward and kissed her.

" Marjorie sorry for papa. Marjorie cry too," the little one said with infinite tenderness.

When Marion returned, Phil went to the door to meet her. He had been watching for her. It had seemed to him he would never see her again. Her absence had been an eternity. One quick glance at him, and she was as pale as death.

"She sees," he said to himself with sinking heart; and then, with a flash of the old will, he forced the gloom away and assumed a cheerful mood.

The next morning he suggested that they should go up to the little rustic summer house on the hill. It was a favorite retreat of theirs, and only a dozen rods from the camp. They had made less than half the distance when he was obliged to stop and rest. They sat down on a bench beside the walk. He had already overtaxed his strength.

It was an effort for Marion to talk. The change that had come over Phil during her absence rent her heart. He had gone to pieces in a day. There was a few moments' silence, and then Phil approached the subject that had brought them there.

"I can't walk so far as I could," he said, his voice quavering slightly. His eyes were fixed upon the dying shrubbery on the other side of the path.

Marion tried to speak. The words choked her. Phil waited a moment, and then went on.

"I cannot shut my eyes, Marion," he said, his voice steadier now. "It is too plain to be misunderstood. I saw it all when you were gone. I had not realized how entirely dependent on you I had become. It was the sound of your voice, the love in your eyes, that kept me up. Without these—without this stimulant that made my life bright, I sank down from utter weakness. After a while I staggered to my feet and looked at myself in the mirror. I was an old man. I knew then what my sunken cheeks meant, Marion—what these wasted hands meant."

Marion tried to hide the emotion that swayed her, but the strain was too great. She broke down and cried like a child, this woman who had been so strong —had been the very life of the man she loved.

Phil tried to comfort her. His words were tender and brave.

"It is merely a day sooner or later, Marion, that is all," he said. "God may have some wise purpose in calling me early. We cannot understand His ways; we cannot understand what tests of moral fiber I shall escape—what sorrow I shall be spared. Death is sometimes kinder than we think."

These last words mingled with the music of Marjorie's voice. She was coming toward them with her nurse. Derringforth looked up and saw her, and a glad smile softened the seriousness of his face. Marion went to meet the little one and took her up in her arms, and brought her to Derringforth, kissing and pressing her to her breast with all a mother's love.

That night Marion and Phil sat alone before the great open fire. A cold November wind swept through the valley. The flames from the blazing pine knots curled, and eddied, and shot up through the chimney with a roar. A fringe of frost had gathered on the window panes.

"This is a winter night," said Marion.

"I wish it were winter in fact," answered Phil.

Marion looked up inquiringly.

"With the trees stripped of their leaves," he went on, "and vegetation dead, I always feel a sense of depression. But when the soft, white snow covers up all this somberness, then the shadows take wings."

They talked for a time, and then there was silence. Their eyes were bent upon the fire. They were thinking.

After a while Marion started up, and went to the window and looked out. The night was very black. She stood there a little while, and with a stifled sigh came back, and drew her chair closer to Phil's. There was a suggestion of irresolution—of hesitation in her manner. Phil looked at her wonderingly. She took a letter from her pocket, and, with unsteady voice, said:

"This will give you a kindlier thought of me, Phil."

"A kindlier thought of you, little girl! No, it is not necessary that I should read it," and he raised his hand in protest.

"There was a time when——"

"But that time has been buried beneath a world of devotion and love," he answered, anticipating what she had started to say. "Let us forget it," he went on; "let me think of you only as the truest friend a man ever had—as the girl I love and have loved all my life."

An expression of unspeakable joy flashed to Marion's face. Phil reached over and took her hand within his own.

"Let me put it in another way, then," she said. "This letter explains something I have wanted you to know. Will you not read it now?"

"Certainly, since you wish it," he answered. "My name," he exclaimed, "and in your writing!" Then he read the various directions on the envelope, and saw the date of the postmark.

His hands trembled as he unfolded the letter. It was the one Marion had sent him just before going to Europe, and which had followed him from New York to Nebraska, and from there to Dakota. His white face became whiter.

"My God! can this be true?" he cried, pressing his hand to his head. He looked at the envelope again, and then at Marion. The room whirled madly. He grasped the arm of his chair. The past rushed back over him like a mighty wave. "My God!" he cried again, "how I wronged you, Marion! Oh, how cruelly I wronged you," and he sank back in his chair, exhausted. It was an overwhelming shock.

Marion was standing over him now, frightened and

pale. "I am so sorry, Phil," she said tenderly. "I should not have shown it to you."

"Yes, you should," he answered, and looked up into her face with a look that cried for forgiveness. The next instant her arms were about him, and the anguish of his soul was stilled by the pressure of her lips upon his. It was an impulse she could not resist—a God inspired impulse that she should not have resisted.

LXXVIII.

It was midnight. Derringforth had not yet fallen asleep. A great, tall, strong man with bronzed and rugged features sat beside him. It was the old guide. He was watching over Derringforth with all the tenderness of a woman ; with all the solicitude of a father by the bedside of his dying boy.

Sometimes Derringforth talked with him, and then, with a far away look in his eyes, he was lost in thought. The room was as unique and pretty as on the night when his eyes first beheld its rustic quaintness. His mind went back to that night, and the emotions that stirred him then again filled his heart.

Dorothy had come back to him in this hour of loneliness, and was bending over him even as he bent over her on that cruel morning in the South when her young life went out. Her eyes were full of tender sympathy, and in the pressure of her hand there was an encouragement and a sense of companionship which did his soul good. He reached up and put his arms around her neck, and brought her face close to his.

"It is all for me, Phil," she whispered, kissing him

just as she used to do. "You sacrificed your life for me, dear," and the tears filled her eyes, and she cried in his arms just as she had once before when a hidden thought of her doom swept over her.

The reverie continued, and by and by Marion came in. In her face, as in Dorothy's, there was tender sympathy. Her eyes were soft with love. Derringforth looked up, and a smile of divine light was on his lips. He stretched out his hand with a thrill of delight, and took hers.

"This is what I have prayed for," he cried with a burst of joy, and he placed Dorothy's hand in Marion's.

The meeting of these two was sweeter than the breath of heaven, and Derringforth was radiantly happy.

The fancy dimmed and was gone. Derringforth turned his head on the pillow, and looked into Jack's face. The old woodsman had been watching him with feverish intentness. He had not moved; had hardly breathed—fearing to break Phil's thoughts. The expression of Derringforth's face had stirred this great, strong man to the depths. There were tears in his eyes when Phil turned toward him.

"You make the world seem sweeter to me, Jack," he said. "I had not supposed that man cared so much for man."

"It's right that he should, it 'pears ter me," answered the old guide, forcing back his emotion.

"The Good Book tells us that God's own Son give up His life fer man."

Derringforth made no answer for a few moments. Finally he looked up and said :

"It gives one a stronger hold on Heaven, Jack, to know such men as you, and to feel the force of your simple, rugged faith. You have done everything for my comfort and happiness since I came up here. I have wondered at your patience with me—at your ceaseless efforts to do for me. Your interest in me has touched me many times, Jack, but never more deeply than tonight. I am glad you are with me. I have wanted to say this to you ; and now, Jack, one thing more. I want you to have my watch—hand it to me, please. I want to give it to you myself—want to see it on you."

Derringforth took the watch, and opening it, saw the time. "It was a present from my father," he said, his lips trembling, his words scarcely audible. He clung to it for a few moments, looking at it in silence. Then he passed it over to the old guide. There were tears in his eyes, and he turned away. Jack started to thank him, but he raised his hand in forbidding gesture.

After a while he fell asleep. Jack still watched over him. It was late when he awoke in the morning. Marion had already been to the room with anxious inquiry. The old woodsman had not yet left him.

"I feel refreshed," Phil said. "I fancied I was a boy again, and my sleep was as sweet as it was then."

He was too weak to dress alone. Jack helped him. He expected to go down to breakfast as usual, but by the time he was ready his strength had failed him. Jack helped him to a chair, and then went down and told Marion. In another minute she was with Derringforth.

"I am so glad you have come," he said, looking up into her eyes with love in his own.

How he had failed since they sat in the firelight together a few hours before! Marion's heart was too full to speak. She bent down and kissed his forehead. He took her hand and raised it to his lips.

"I am so sorry I left you at all last night," she said tenderly.

"But it was my wish," he answered. "I could not have allowed you to sit up; and besides, it was not necessary. I slept like a child, and dreamed I was a boy again, and that I could ride and row and jump and tumble just as I used to do. And you were with me, Marion, and the sport we had will keep my heart young." He had almost added, "throughout the ages ahead," but stopped suddenly.

He was sufficiently rested now to go into the adjoining room while his own was put in order. Then he returned and tried to eat a bit of breakfast.

"It looks very tempting," he said, "but I don't feel that I could swallow a morsel."

"Jack cooked the trout," said Marion.

Derringforth had already motioned the tray away.

"Dear old fellow," he said, "I must eat, then;" and he did—not much, but yet enough to gladden the old guide's heart.

After a while Derringforth lay down on the couch. He asked for Marjorie. The nurse brought her in, and left her alone with Marion and Phil. The child stood by her father, and looked at him with mature intelligence. Her face was very sad. His arm was about her; and the expression of his eyes told that he realized they would look upon her but a few hours more. He looked up at Marion and said:

"I wish that I might live to see her grow up—to give her a father's love and care."

Tears were stealing down his cheeks. Marion took Marjorie in her arms, and drew up close to Phil. He talked with her about the child's future, and the plans he had made for her.

"They shall be carried out faithfully," said Marion, choking back the sobs.

A servant came up and handed Marion a telegram. "It is from Mrs. Rayburn," she said, with a sigh of relief. "She will be here this afternoon."

"I am so glad," answered Phil. "I was afraid she would not get here."

Marion shuddered. He saw the tremor, and quickly added, "today—get here today."

About ten o'clock Marion looked toward the window. The air was filled with flying snow flakes. "Oh, Phil," she cried, "your snow has come."

"So it has," he answered, a look of delight coming into his face, and he raised himself on his arm.

Marion placed a large easy chair by the glass doors, and then helped Phil into it. He watched the falling snow with keen interest. The lake had frozen over, and already a great white sheet stretched far out before him. The ground and the trees were soon covered, and all the evidences of the dying year were hidden. "I never saw the world so beautiful before," he said. "How soft and pure and peaceful it all is!"

Marjorie was playing on the great bear skin rug. She had already forgotten to be sad. Derringforth turned his head and looked down at her, and a smile lighted up his face as he saw her happy with her toys. He watched her for some moments, and then turned back toward the window to look again at the falling snow and out over the lake and across to the tall trees, now a great bank of white, rising far up in the heavens. Marion's chair was beside him. He reached out and took her hand.

"I have been thinking," he said, "what a beautiful world God has given us. I have never seen it as I see it now," and his eyes disclosed the pathetic cry of his soul for life.

Very soon after this he was compelled to give up and go to bed. Mrs. Rayburn was due at three. He followed the hands of the clock. His will alone was keeping him up. Marion was beside him. He was too low to talk much, but finally he looked up into her eyes, and tightening the pressure on her hand, he said:

"I wish I might live, Marion, to make you happy —to be well again and love you as only a well, strong man can love. I would give you my life, my devotion. You have given these to me, and how badly I have repaid you! It was all a cruel mistake, Marion —cruel fate. God alone knows what we have both suffered. One wrong move, and everything is changed. The penalty sometimes seems severe."

A knock at the door; Marion turned her head. Jack had come to say that Mrs. Rayburn was just driving up. Phil's face brightened.

"You must go to meet her," he said to Marion, his voice scarcely above a whisper. But even yet he clung to her hand, a look of boundless yearning in his eyes.

"I will be gone only a minute," she said; "Jack will stay with you."

She got as far as the door and came back, why she knew not. She threw her arms about him and kissed him. He looked up with a smile of infinite joy. "Go fetch grandma now," he whispered.

Jack bent over him. He tried to speak. His eyes

dimmed. The old woodsman, with tears streaming down his cheeks, ran to meet Marion. She flew to the bedside.

Again Derringforth had left Marion to join Dorothy.

www.ingramcontent.com/pod-product-compliance
Lightning Source LLC
Chambersburg PA
CBHW020757230426
43666CB00007B/741